RUNNING
WITH
GOD

RUNNING WITH GOD

GREG VICK

credo
house publishers

Published in the United States of America by Credo House Publishers,
a division of Credo Communications LLC, Grand Rapids, Michigan
credohousepublishers.com

ISBN: 978-1-62586-171-9

Cover and interior design by Sharon VanLoozenoord
Editing by Pete Ford

Printed in the United States of America

First edition

*To God's presence in my life
and in the lives of our children and their spouses,
Kevin and Ann, Kerry and Jill,
Adam and Nicki, and Sara and Gustavo.
May they continue to nurture our grandchildren
with His Holy Spirit.*

CONTENTS

INTRODUCTION

"We need to take him to the hospital," were the first words I heard when I woke up. God's response was, *Not this man, not today!* Even though my body had just suffered through a great deal of trauma, when I awakened, there was such a high level of relief and overall healthy welfare surrounding me, that I knew God was in control, and I was ready to get out of that place. And I've been "running" with God ever since.

It was July 4, 2006, and I was in Atlanta, Georgia, participating in the world's largest 10K race (6.2 miles with 55,000 runners and walkers) called the Peachtree Road Race. I use the term 'participating' loosely, since I finished the race in a horizontal posture, rather than the preferred vertical.

When I regained consciousness, I was surrounded by ice packs strategically placed around my body. I ran the race in approximately 68 minutes and spent about 70 minutes in the infirmary. The day started as a festive holiday and almost ended with a not-so-festive hospital visit. *Certainly, this is not the way running—and life in general—are supposed to go! Who wants to spend Independence Day with dependence on a medical staff?* Not to mention the anguish my brother Terry told me he had, watching me lying unconscious and motionless on an army cot in the med tent. He was there because he and another "kind soul" stopped running their races, saw me collapsed on the pavement, picked me up, and carried me across the finish line and immediately into the spacious, outdoor, first aid station.

Living in the Atlanta area for a long time and having run this annual race on multiple occasions, my brother was ecstatic that year that I had finally accepted his annual offer to run the Peachtree with him. Living in northeastern Indiana, it was not an easy decision for me to drop my responsibilities and simply come south and run this longtime special race, which had its debut in 1970.

But in 2006 I said, "Yes," to his offer, cleared space on my weekly calendar for the trip and race, and planned to have an enjoyable experience with my seven-year-younger brother. However, God had His plan as well, which included several lessons for me to absorb on the "learning and running curve of life." I had not prepared properly for this event in any of the three main aspects of balanced living, mental, physical, and spiritual, that I now consider profoundly important.

God had been a presence in my life, at some level, for many years. But since I started running with a purpose and actually logging miles of training, which was new to me, I had not "connected the dots" yet, to open up my running life to include Him.

RUNNING
WITH
GOD

FINDING GOD

Christmas Magic

I grew up as a kid in the 1950s, and all things Mickey Mouse were trending. (And still are almost 70 years later!) For those few who didn't like Mickey, there was Minnie Mouse too. As most of us know, there are still several "sidekicks" who share the cartoon scene with Mickey and Minnie. I guess I was in the minority of those who liked the Mickey Mouse brand but preferred one of the "extras." I liked Donald Duck, perhaps, because he wasn't the "star of the show." Yet today, I have a deep appreciation for the "underdogs" in life.

Anyway, my Christmas wish list at age seven consisted of one item: a Donald Duck stuffed toy. The problem for me (way) back then was that boys wore blue clothes and played baseball and other sports, and girls wore pink and played with dolls and such. And I thought my dream gift might be considered a doll.

It was a stuffed toy with duck features that was about two feet tall. It included Donald's face and beak, dressed in a sailor's uniform. Because I thought it might be in the doll category, I didn't tell a soul about my Christmas wishes, not my parents, siblings, grandparents, or friends, not even Santa Claus when I sat on his knee at a department store!

Bedtime on Christmas Eve was usually past midnight, as our family annually attended a late-night candlelight service at our local Methodist church. I remember, when I went to bed around 12:30 on Christmas morning, that in addition to my usual night-time prayers, there was another hope, that the one and only wish item I had might be under the tree in the morning? It was, for sure, a distant hope, since I still hadn't told anyone my true Christmas wish.

At some point during my early morning sleep, an upper-body image of Jesus became very vivid and distinctive to me. It was not merely a passing thought, as the mind has a tendency to do at times, rambling from one notion to another. It also was not a brief five- or ten-second thought either. It seemed to last the duration of my sleep! It definitely had a purpose, as only two words were spoken, *"Follow me."* This message from Jesus was immensely impactful, especially for a seven-year-old. The image and spoken words concluded my morning's sleep, and I woke up.

Having grown up with fairy tales, magic wands, and special effects, I was aware of elements that could "touch" a person in some way. But this moment presented an indescribable sensation within me and over my body, like a special blessing that I was privileged to receive. And this happened on Christmas morning from Jesus himself! My Christmas was complete and had reached the pinnacle of "best Christmas ever"! After I absorbed all that had meaningfully taken place that early morning, I left my bedroom with a feeling of euphoric energy and headed to the living room and our Christmas tree.

Shockingly, in front of our usually natural and decorated fir was the stuffed Donald Duck toy for which I had hoped. Absolutely, I could not believe what I saw. Always being a contemplator and sometimes an over-analyzer, I tried to process what took place, thinking, *Wow, Jesus, somehow You made this happen!* As a youngster, I had additional thoughts like, *Jesus, did You talk to Santa Claus?* and *Wow, Jesus, You must be more powerful than Santa Claus!*

Those Jesus and Christmas moments are permanently etched in my essence, and I've been following Jesus ever since. If I got anything else as a gift that day, it was totally not remembered or noticed. I was oblivious to everything else, as I had Jesus, Donald, and Christmas all on the same day! Life at age seven couldn't be any better!

"Jesus called out to them, 'Come, follow me.'"

MARK 1:17

Meaningful Pictures

When my grandpa on my mom's side of the family passed away, I was given a wallet-sized remembrance card of his life. Since he had been such an important influence on me in many ways during my growing up, I saved the card. Another reason I cherished that card, and still do today, is that on the opposite side is a picture of Jesus, as Grandpa was a devoted man of faith. The third reason why I still have this small memento almost forty years later is that the image of Jesus is exactly like the one I saw during my spiritual Christmas Eve sleep at the age of seven. Even though that small rectangular card has tattered edges and corners now, both sides of it represent an abundance of deep-seated meaning for me.

Another keepsake, of the few that have earned a lasting place in my wallet, is a snapshot taken by a Kodak camera about fifty years ago. It is a picture showing a mountainous area with a wide swath of dense clouds looming over the peaks. When you look closely at the photo, there is a faint single ray of sunshine that sneaks through the turbulent-looking gray and white clouds. Despite the ominous look of impending weather, of greatest significance to me was that within the cloud structure, at that moment in time, was one of the images of what Jesus' face might have looked like. To me, the image and thin ray of light represent God's presence today in the "heart" of any "storms" of life. This photo has also aged and continues to stay in my wallet.

Early Years

Even though God's presence was a dramatic moment early in my life, trying to understand exactly what that meant was still somewhat of a mystery to be solved. To help support the family of seven, Dad Harry worked both a full-time day job at one of the local steel mills and a part-time job on some evenings and Saturdays at a large retail store. He also did catalogue shoe sales to supplement the family income. It was easy to understand, then, that his time on Sundays was frequently needed for rest and recuperation. Therefore, Mom Lois was the one to make sure we went to church on Sunday mornings. It was also important to her that we each had a contribution to put in the collection basket at our Sunday School classes, usually a nickel or dime. I do remember learning about Jesus at those many Sunday settings. The church service that followed was primarily for adults, so we rarely attended, unless there was a special occasion, or if Dad came on that Sunday and could help with supervising us kids in the pew.

Elementary Years

In elementary school, I remember a couple of impactful stories. At the age of ten, I came close to drowning in the lake after which the town was named, Cedar Lake. I didn't know how to swim yet, but I was enticed by other friends to go 20 or 25 feet from the pier to a large floating raft, where all my friends were playing. Each step took me deeper and deeper as the water level continued to climb higher above my shoulders. Only, about ten feet from the platform, loaded with my "buddies," my head went totally under water. Then somehow I was able to "bounce" off the lake bottom only for a moment, to get part of my head above water, before gaspingly going under again. I recall feeling "doomed" at that point.

Fortunately, one of the boys, a nine-year-old, must have seen me go under and came off the wooden raft and pulled me up. He then held on and guided me back to the safety of the pier. I will always remember the name of that boy, Cecil, who was a life saver on that day, but I also had a sense then that God had a hand in that episode. Minimally, I believe, He gave an urging to my friend to come rescue me.

Another story from my elementary days took place in my fourth grade public school classroom. Our teacher was, I believe, the oldest educator in the building and was quite the traditionalist. She believed in incorporating Bible study into our regular curriculum, and to my knowledge, was the only educator in the building who did that. Out of respect, I will only mention her first name, Ethyl. Regardless of anybody's background or religious preference, Miss Ethyl "made" us learn Bible verses, in addition to her sharing of Scriptures and their interpretation. The biblical portion of our day was immediately after our lunch and recess break, every Monday through Friday.

She gave us a short message from the Bible each day, in addition to a Scripture lesson. In unison, our class said the Scripture together. Every Friday, then, was recitation time. When we returned from our lunch break, all students stood by their chairs. No one was allowed to sit down until he or she recited from memory a particular Scripture verse that was assigned to that person earlier in the week. Those who struggled with memorization were still standing for a while, even after our regular afternoon curriculum began. They could continue to look at their Scripture notes until their recitation was complete. Trust me, being one of the "standers," now and then, was no fun at all! Even though I was not quick to learn those verses then, and I stood longer than I wanted at times, later in life, I respected her more, because of her convictions and efforts to introduce God's Word to so many. *Thank You, God, for Miss Ethyl!*

Elementary education had a lot of liberties back in the 1950s. Remember the phrase, "Spare the rod, spoil the child?" In my public-school setting, there were examples that I witnessed where a student's "misbehavior" earned a ruler smack across the hand or knuckles. And if someone was more "out-of-line," he or she got a backseat whack from a paddle right in front of the room, in clear view of the other students. Another discipline strategy used then was for a student to stand at the back of the room facing a wall or blackboard with a piece of chewed gum stuck between that person's nose tip and the vertical structure. Oh, to be a kid again! Or not?

Teen Years

During my teenage years, I remember living in a different city and attending another Methodist church. I went to Sunday School there regularly and to a church service more often. As time went on, I added the church youth group (MYF— Methodist Youth Fellowship) to my routine each Sunday evening. At this Methodist church in Hammond, Indiana, I was more engaged in my faith learning.

I remember reciting several creeds and doctrines and singing a number of hymns of faith on a regular basis, nearly every Sunday morning. But I never had a totally clear concept what their content meant. The phrase "God in three persons" was a nebulous term to me then. Since we spoke, read, and sang those words so often, I felt embarrassed to ask the question of my Sunday School teacher, another church member, or even my parents. So, despite my frequent attendance at church, I still didn't understand fully some of the core concepts of our church and my faith.

College Years

During my college years, I attended the campus Methodist Church sporadically, as Sunday mornings were frequently needed to "catch-up" on sleep after a full week of classes and other student activities. Additionally, to help financially, I was on a work-study program which required more time and effort throughout each week. I certainly was thankful that I could experience the total college scene and had the opportunity to work on campus. But unfortunately, I wasn't able to attend the church setting more often to, hopefully, add to my spiritual growth.

To help finance my college expenses more, I worked four summers, and sometimes during my Christmas and semester breaks, in one of the local steel mills in northwestern Indiana. Because I was a temporary employee, I experienced a wide variety of job assignments. During some weeks, I did something different each day. Some of those jobs were the dirtiest, sweatiest, most physical, and most dangerous tasks I've ever done in my life! Each helped me mature and learn a great deal about my circumstances and the world around me. This also helped me appreciate my college education and look forward to returning to school each fall.

Also, for the first time in my life, I experienced my mind, body, and spirit adjusting to shift-work. During one summer, we changed eight-hour shifts every week. We rotated from the day shift one week (starting at 7 a.m.) to the evening shift the next week (starting at 3 p.m.) and then to the midnight shift (starting at 11 p.m.). For me, it was quite the challenge, as it generally took my body and sleeping patterns three to five days to get used to the new shift. Then a couple days later it was on to the next rotation.

While there were a few instances during those steel mill years where a body part—usually a finger, hand, or arm—would get a little bump, bruise, or scratch, I felt and needed God's presence a couple times, and not simply as a band-aid. With Him "on board" during two instances, I survived potentially severe or fatal injuries. Neither was caused by any negligence on anyone's part, but rather low percentage circumstances just happened, and I was in harm's way to possibly bear the consequences.

On one of those occasions, I was penned into an outside area without the ability to move. A massive dump truck loaded with hot, molten refuse slag from an open-hearth mill was backing up towards me to release its load. Because of the emergency sound coming from the back-up system of the truck and the steam coming from previous debris dumps, the driver could neither hear my yells nor see me. Behind me was a cliff-like, jagged rock drop-off of 15 or 20 feet, which helped form a wall for Lake Michigan. I had no options and no control of the situation. There were probably four different scenarios that could have taken place, and realistically, only one that would keep me alive. After the driver and truck concluded their mission and drove away, still with no idea that I was there, I walked out of that situation amazed and said, *Thank You, God! There must be a reason why You want me to continue on.*

Author's note: In case you are wondering how I got into that predicament, it was my job on that day. I was a "spotter" with the assignment of helping trucks loaded with steel mill waste, to back up safely and deposit their large pile of hot refuse as close to the Lake Michigan edge as possible. Then days later, a bulldozer would push all the piles into the lake, as a part of the steel mill's expansion of land surface into the Great Lake. The "truckers" were instructed to follow my safe guidance while backing up. They were also told that if there were no spotter present, then they were to dump their load on their own cautiously. So, while I had solely spotted one truck and was standing a foot or two from that steamy hot load, a second truck arrived and followed his protocol, which put me in a challenging dilemma.

I definitely felt God's guiding hand and His nearness to me on many occasions during those college maturation moments. I said those three familiar words, *Thank You, God!*, on many occasions, especially when I made some poor decisions from time to time. I was in college because I sensed He wanted me there. Attending college right out of high school looked like an extremely bleak possibility at the time. I was interested in pursuing a teaching career, but family finances were not conducive for that. Then, unexpectedly, an inheritance of $2,000 from a deceased grandma came at the right time for me to enroll in college. When that amount was added to my summer work income, I had enough to start the first semester. Otherwise, there might not have been a college career for me, or at least it would not have started the year I graduated from high school.

> *"God has perfect timing; never early, never late.*
> *It takes a little patience and it takes*
> *a lot of faith but it's worth the wait."*
> ANONYMOUS

Career Time

I also felt God's guiding hand in directing and encouraging me in my career choices. Back in my junior high school days, when I wrote a career research paper on the topic of teaching, I sensed that He favored my intentions to help the younger generation through teaching and coaching education. I entered college to be a secondary high school instructor and sports coach. As if God was nodding His head and saying, *Yes*, I always felt comfortable with those choices throughout my four college years. I graduated in May 1972 and I was hired the next month to start my professional career that August.

With God's help, my assignments seemed to fit the talents He gave me and the training I had received. I spent my entire 33-year career teaching and coaching at the same high school. I was blessed with the rare opportunity to not have to "bounce around" from job to job.

Was I "bored" with a "one-stop" career? Heavens, no! God provided me with unique, complementary challenges along the way, which were also extremely rewarding. As a high school foreign language (German) instructor for all 33 years, I was able to contribute to the growth of the program from less than 40 students in my first year to nearly 300 when I retired. On 11 occasions I led many of my students and some of their parents on adventures to Europe.

My coaching experiences afforded me opportunities in four different sports, with a minimum of five years per sport. Additionally, I coached at every high school level possible, from Assistant Freshmen, to Head Freshmen, to Assistant Junior Varsity, all the way up to Head Varsity. Getting a chance to coach both boys' and girls' sports, to me, was also a blessing designed and led by God's hand.

Because of my coaching background in a wide variety of sports, I was given the opportunity to sportscast high school sports for the local radio and TV station. This unexpected part-time job started out as a one game broadcasting sampler that expanded over time, to total nearly 1,600 games in 14 boys' and girls' sports over a 20-year period. Complementing that during the same time, I hosted a special sports talk interview show with area coaches and players on Saturday mornings for around 45 weeks of each calendar year. For sure, I "never saw that one coming," especially for a person who was not trained in the field of broadcasting!

God did, and He put me where He wanted me to do His work. Without a doubt, God not only urged me to do my teaching, coaching, and broadcasting careers concurrently during those remarkably busy 20 years, but He also gave me the physical, mental, and spiritual strength to do all of those assignments. *How did I know He was involved?* Because at the end of each day, no matter how late it was, sometimes at midnight or beyond, I prayed to Him before I went to sleep. Every prayer started with, "Thank You, God, for the opportunities, challenges, and experiences I had today to help others the best I could." Somewhere in each prayer was, "Give me the strength and stamina, Your leadership and guidance, and the courage and wisdom to handle those matters tomorrow that You want me to do, when I interact with those You send to me."

There were absolutely no second thoughts. God was "driving the bus" and "orchestrating" my days. Depending on variables such as where I coached a volleyball match on a Thursday night and where I did a football game broadcast on a Friday night, I had some long days of eighteen to twenty hours of activity with only four to six hours of sleep. I would describe that as "running on fumes," with an impending breakdown of some sort imminent.

Honestly, I kept waiting for my "fumes" to run out on any given day, but they never did! Here and there, I had two or three of those days in a row, and I wondered in amazement, *How is all this happening at a seemingly, high level of performance?* For me, I was "running" on God's strength and will. He supplied what I *needed*. With all my responsibilities, I was "doing my best and letting God do the rest." I sensed that I was doing what He wanted me to do, and for Him, I was the right guy at the right time to do it. From my experience, it seemed unbelievable that, physically, I felt as rejuvenated after only a few hours of sleep that normally would have taken eight to ten hours of rest to accomplish.

So let's not get tired of doing what is good . . .
we will reap a harvest of blessing if we don't give up.
GALATIANS 6:9

To me, the mental, physical, spiritual, and emotional strength necessary to do what I was doing could only have one source: God. Certainly, some fitness factors helped my stamina, but the quantity of obligations I had and the level of quality that others and I expected of my performances made for an extremely active lifestyle.

Sometimes I prayed that if God wanted me to do something different or better, He would give me the guidance necessary. Usually, it was a thought that popped into my head, frequently in the early morning before I awakened or started my day. Pursuing that notion almost always made for a better day for someone.

Back then, and even now on some days, I said to Him, "God, I think I know what You want me to do right now, but for me to accomplish that, I think I need a little help." The assistance has come in a variety of ways. On occasion, an unexpected person enters the room, one who can help me through my dilemma. Sometimes, I get an urge or thought to ask someone from whom I hadn't considered seeking help. There were times when I was transporting something important for someone and a heavy wind or rain developed that might damage it.

At such a time, I requested better travel conditions, so the recipient would not get a tainted product.

If I needed a thought from a different perspective about how to do something more easily or more efficiently, I requested some help. If I didn't receive an answer, I carried on in the same manner as I was doing, realizing that that was my answer. Through no apparent answer, God was saying, *Your thought pattern and procedure is the most efficient way right now*, or, *Continue on, you need this challenge right now as experience to help you in the future.*

> **"'For I know the plans I have for you,'
> says the Lord. 'They are plans for good and not for disaster,
> to give you a future and a hope.'"**
> JEREMIAH 29:11

In God's Hands

At our previous house where we lived for 30 years, we had a substantial amount of tree-related work due to several mature trees, each over 50 years old. The trimming of branches that hung over the house was one such project. About ten years ago, one of those "strong arms" of one of our front yard trees had grown horizontally about 35 feet away from its trunk. It extended to the edge of our neighbor's property and beyond it to the other side of their driveway.

Then one day, hearing that our neighbor was in the early process of selling her house, I decided to cut off most of that branch myself, so a prospective buyer could see all of our neighbor's house. From an extension ladder, my eye level and the location of the cut were 17 feet off the ground. While the branch ran east and west, I faced south for the right-handed cut, well away from the ladder. Also facing south and behind me, my wife Cathy assisted by holding a taut rope to ensure that the branch did not swing into the neighbor's house.

With all variables accounted for and calculations in place, including padding on the ground where the branch would land, we proceeded. However, as the branch came towards the ground, it fell into the ladder, which buckled into two pieces and took away my stability. As Cathy observed the branch, two ladder pieces, and her husband falling through the air, something unique about that fall caught her attention.

Time seemed to stand still for a brief moment or two. In mid-air my body made a 90-degree, quarter turn to land facing west. I landed in a seated position with bent knees, instead of being stretched out horizontally. Significantly, this tree had deep and extensive spiderweb-type roots right beside me, some of which protruded above the ground up to four inches high. Landing between those roots and in that position, prevented not only my head, neck, spine, and tailbone from potentially severe injuries, but also possible hip, knee, and ankle issues as well.

From Cathy's view, she said, "It looked like you were 'caught' in the air, turned to the side and gently placed down on your seat." Our only explanation is that, directly or indirectly, God had a hand in this experience. We both were blessed with the results of this tree episode. I did sustain a couple minor injuries that healed up normally without any pain medication. *Thank You, God, for all of the above!*

> **"What joy for those whose strength comes from the Lord."**
>
> PSALM 84:5

FINDING RUNNING

2

Rookie Runner

My teenage years were in the 1960s in northwest Indiana, an area noted for its steel mills and referred to as the "Region." I grew up alongside younger brothers, Mike, Terry, Tim, and Doug. While growing up, our sport of choice was baseball. We played it often, especially since our dad enjoyed coaching us in the summers at the Little League and Babe Ruth levels, basically ages nine to fifteen. Depending on interest here and there, some basketball, football, and tennis were sprinkled in for us boys as well. I added volleyball during my college years, since it wasn't available at our high school, and a couple of us played some golf and softball as we got older.

In brief, I was surrounded by and enjoyed the hand-eye and foot-eye coordination activities, which I call the "ball sports." (Of note, back then soccer was considered a totally "foreign" sport, played by foreigners, in foreign countries.) Running? That was foreign, too, at least to me! It was a concept I only did to perform my ball sports skills and when a coach with a whistle motivationally "made" other teammates and me do some conditioning sprints before and after practice!

But running as a sport or for recreation? No way that was happening, even though our high school offered teams for Cross Country in the fall and Track and Field in the spring. With my participation at some level with football in the fall, basketball in the winter, and baseball in the spring and summer, my sports life was pretty full. So, running long distances or sprinting short distances was simply not "on my radar" for time or participation. Even during my 33-year professional career of high school teaching and coaching, the sports I coached were from the same genre—the ball sports of football, basketball, baseball, and volleyball.

So, what inspired me to take up running? As stated in my previous book, *Mastering the Moments: Life Lessons Inspired by a Tai Chi Master* (2018), my master-instructor-mentor influenced me in many areas of life, including running. He was an avid long-distance runner, sometimes running seven miles during his lunch hour break. He prepared for marathons, some overseas, and logged over 48,000 miles during his approximate, 25-year running career.

Master Robert Sbarge of my hometown of Auburn, Indiana, passed away in July 2005. Among other matters, he inspired me with his dedication to running, sometimes at temperatures in the 90-degree Fahrenheit range. Soon after his passing I made running a committed part of my life. Still today, 15 years later, I dedicate one of my miles of each race to my mentor.

When I began to take up running, it was only at a minimal level, a few tenths of a mile going north on Iwo Street, located about one mile east of downtown Auburn. After a short distance, I turned around and headed back south to McIntyre Drive, where I lived. With experience over time, I added some distance going east on the intersecting 7th Street and eventually, ran south on Duesenberg Drive. By turning west, back onto McIntyre, I was able to complete a rectangular route of about one and a half miles. Here and there, I added a short side street or cul-de-sac in our immediate neighborhood.

Almost exactly one year after my mentor's passing, I ran my first race, following his inspiration. Since I had been playing morning pick-up basketball a couple times a week with a few fellow teachers and coaches, I felt this conditioning and my recent beginning into committed running would be enough training to carry me through the Atlanta race. Oh, did I miscalculate that one! I definitely displayed my "rookie" runner status!

Peach Challenge

For that hot, humid race day climate on July 4 in Atlanta, Georgia, I wore my black, high-top, heavy basketball shoes, instead of light-weight runner's shoes. Additionally, my choice of wearing apparel consisted of heavier cotton items rather than light-weight, quick-drying, wicking materials. Also, I was not a "hat guy" at the beginning of my running career, to shield off the sun, nor did I know anything about the benefits of wearing compression socks to keep good blood flow through those valuable legs and feet.

Another reason (yes, there's more) was my poor preparation with regards to proper hydration in those southern conditions. I even thought that my conditioning was so good that I could "skip" some of the water stations to save some time on the course! During the 6.2-mile race there were five race-official hydration stops, featuring water and sports drink options. There were also a couple other water-only stops, usually sponsored by local churches to "donate" to the cause by assisting 55,000 runners and walkers. Since I didn't even know what a water belt was (to carry your own water bottles), my body was totally dependent on what water I got at the stations. As I recall, I only stopped twice for water, and I certainly did not adequately hydrate during this race. All of these factors were a recipe for disaster! Even worse than all of that, God was not a part of my running game plan at that stage of my life. He was a part of my life, but not my running life.

Dedicated runners reading this account can probably predict what happened during that race. Without adequate hydration for the body and with electrolytes sweating out of my system, along with the high heat, humidity, and hills of this race taking their toll, my body started "breaking down" at the five-mile marker. As I continued running, more areas of the body were compromised and "squeaked" their displeasure. Being the complete rookie runner, I did not realize that my dilemma was a water issue. Even if I did, there were no more water stops on the course. Unfortunately, my competitive nature kept saying, *You are almost there. You can do this.*

A portion of the last half mile was downhill, so I thought I could make it and I continued on, actually speeding up due to the hill decline. However, I was definitely running too fast for my circumstances. About 20 yards from the finish line I had to make a quick adjustment, so that I didn't run over a person in front of me who had suddenly stopped, thinking she had crossed the finish line. That was what I heard her say to a friend on her right. At a fast pace, I tried to step to my left to avoid contact, but in so doing, I broke stride and my body collapsed like a "bag of bones." My left knee hit the pavement and "out" I went, totally unconscious. I remembered no other details of the race. Approximately 55 minutes later, thankfully, God intervened, and He's been a major part of my running ever since. And so has proper training, hydration, footwear, and clothing!

Post-Race

To be sure, I learned a lot from that first Atlanta race experience. I was so thankful that, health-wise, there was a good ending with no apparent, lingering physical or mental shortcomings that would negatively affect my life or running going forward, except for the scar on my left knee. My brother Terry—who was deeply concerned while watching me in the med tent and had thoughts like, "Why did I invite him at his age of 56 to take on this racing challenge in the South?"—recovered as well. But going forward, he has reminded me and other family members, to my chagrin, how he carried me across the finish line of that race. Naturally, he has the opportunity to embellish the story to whatever level he wishes, since no other family members were present. So, I am totally stuck with his portrayal of the saga every time!

Although the race itself had a rough ending for me, the recovery was complete, and my sense of God's presence, to me at least, was real and meaningful. Following that Atlanta episode, I felt I needed to include God in my running from that point on. He was there when I needed Him the most, and He and I needed to do this running adventure together. My training methods needed alteration as well.

HONORING GOD'S PRESENCE

3

Day of the Son/Sun

Ever since I dedicated myself to distance running, I made a Sunday run a part of my weekly routine. For twelve years of my running career, I was blessed that our church had a Saturday evening service. Cathy and I totally enjoyed that Saturday option at our local Dayspring Community Church in Auburn, Indiana. Also, the time and length of service suited us well. The start time was 6 p.m. with a targeted end time of one hour later.

With that logistic, there was still adequate time for a "date night" supper at a local restaurant. Also, for me, this service provided not only the opportunity to be available to run on Sunday mornings, but also the spiritual carry-over from the message, prayer, thoughts, song lyrics, and, of course, God's Word from the evening before. I carried this inspiration with me into the next morning, when I did my solo runs with God, which were usually my longest runs of the week.

Even though our church dropped the Saturday evening gathering from its schedule a couple years ago, the Sunday morning run is still a major part of my running routine. Now I wake up a little earlier on Sundays and do my "Day of the Sun Fun Run" and finish in enough time to cool-down, stretch, and clean-up before attending church. When we are visiting family out-of-town or state, I am able to still do my "Day of the Son Fun Run" with God most of the time before family members are up and about. I like to interchange the words, "sun," and "son," depending on where I want to put more emphasis that day. Both are spiritual concepts to me. Sun represents natural light and the gift from God of a new day. Also, it refers to the seventh day of the week or Sabbath. Son reminds me of God's Son, Jesus, and all that He represents.

Five Mottos

Happy moments, praise God
Difficult moments, seek God
Quiet moments, worship God
Painful moments, trust God
Every moment, thank God
RICK WARREN, Pastor and Author

I'm not sure when I came across this analogy, but it truly impacts me deeply, especially during my runs. I can say from experience that on every run, short or long, slow or fast, competitive or not, at least four of those situations occur. The one that doesn't always occur would be the fourth scenario on the list, referring to pain. If pain existed on each of my three runs weekly, I'm sure I would move on from this activity and choose something else for recreation, fitness and spiritual development.

Trusting

For sure, there have been many uncomfortable moments when I've had to rest and not run for a few days or a week or two. Sometimes, I even had to bypass a race I had planned to run and was committed to financially. Actually, in those moments, I felt I turned a negative situation into a positive one. I put my trust in God that He provided the challenge that I needed at that moment. Sometimes I sensed His message was, *Greg, you have over-trained recently and some of your body parts need additional rest, rather than "ramping up" for the next race.* Even though all my races have non-refundable fees attached to them, it is still a good feeling, that at least I donated to a substantially worthwhile cause. For some of my races, the donation to the local sponsoring organization is my higher priority, and the race itself is simply a "bonus."

The only exception to this protocol was in 2017, when I planned and paid for my most expensive race, which was several states away in Georgia. During my late winter and early spring training I developed a deep heel and arch discomfort on my right foot called plantar fasciitis. Since I had not experienced this older-age malady that many runners and non-runners get, I didn't know I had the problem until it was deeply imbedded. According to experienced runners I knew, what took a long time to develop was going to take a long time to heal. There was a degree of discomfort every time my right foot hit the pavement during every run.

Since my foot issue did not affect other areas of the body, I minimized my training significantly and continued to do everything recommended by experts. In addition to a new insole for my shoe, I began experimenting with different types of sponge padding that I could use to lessen the impact of every right foot pavement strike. On race day I decided to use three layers of sponge material to complement the structured insole. My trust was totally with God as I crossed the start line to begin the race and said, "With You, God, let's do this together!" I trusted Him to help me navigate through this special race.

Still today, I totally enjoy the challenge of that unique race in Atlanta, Georgia, called the Peachtree Road Race. It offers heat, humidity, and hills (the three h's, as the Atlantans refer to it) on July Fourth. That year I had the extra burden of the right foot issue for every other step of the 6.2 miles of mostly inclined and declined running. With God, the insole, the spongy layers, and some natural race-time adrenaline, I was able to complete the race with a respectable time.

Throughout any given race, when certain body parts tweak their disapproval of their circumstances, I rely on God's guiding hand to help me make the proper adjustments necessary to keep me going as efficiently as possible. *Do I need to change my stride or pace? Should I consider walking a bit? Do I need to stop and stretch out a body part? Do I need more or less nutrition and hydration than I planned at this stage of the race?* If it appears to be a struggle to get to the finish line, I remind myself what I said at the start line: "With You, God."

Whether the body is aching or fatiguing, or if my pace and stride are still smooth, near the end of a race, I try to put a final "kick" in, to finish the race as strongly as possible. Regardless of conditions, for the last quarter of a mile or so, I say to myself, "Trust God, just do it." Then I focus on that phrase and belief and try to totally relax the entire body. I put complete faith in Him that He will see me to and through that day's finish line. Additionally, I have confidence that any recuperation or healing necessary going forward in life will be in His caring hands.

"Trust in the Lord with all your heart."

PROVERBS 3:5

Praising

Frequently, when I leave the house for a run, Cathy will ask, "How far or long are you running today?" Almost always, I give her my goal with a quantifier, "It depends on how the body parts respond after the warm-up and transition to running." Initially, when I leave our driveway and enter my first street of the day, I praise God for the opportunity to be healthy enough to put on the appropriate running clothes by myself and am able, at least, to start a walking journey on that day. I never take those circumstances for granted, as I have friends and relatives, in my age group, who are physically unable to walk or run at this moment. When I acknowledge this, I feel blessed, and I try to make the most of what God has given me at that moment. My smile and the happiness I feel inside, knowing He is with me, give me and my body a sense of relaxation, which I know will help my performance.

When I run, I try to be aware of my surroundings at all times. My running world consists of so many interesting, unique, and seemingly miraculous elements. It is transcendent, for the most part, how every item seems to fit together harmoniously. The natural settings of fields and forests give beauty, at least to me, and function for property owners and animals and other creatures, large and small, flying or otherwise. Modernization and implementation of construction has brought about streets, sidewalks, and houses that have turned into family communities. In some areas, people have had to share their space with the living creatures who once used that area when no humans existed there. I praise God that He blends all this together, and I get to enjoy both the old and the new, and many times, the mixture of the two. I am blessed when I can run and enjoy nature at the same time.

Seeking

Finding challenges in running is never a problem. They find me, *easily!* Moment-by-moment and step-by-step circumstances present changing conditions throughout any training run or race. Some are as simple as re-tying a shoelace, even though it started out with a double knot, or needing to drink or eat something. Other issues revolve around temperature, wind, precipitation, and elevation, in addition to running elements such as posture, pace, and stride length. At the other end of the spectrum are body parts, usually the legs, that have some level of aching, that let me know they are not pleased with the way matters are going at that moment.

When those difficult moments arise, I seek God's help. *Thank You, God, for the experiences so far, but now I've got a very challenging problem and I need Your help.* For example, a tightness in a calf or hamstring muscle can lead to several responses.

Do I continue at the same pace for a short bit of time and see if it will warm-up more and take care of itself? Do I slow down my pace or alter my stride and hope for an improved scenario? Do I stop completely and do some additional stretching? Do I stop and only walk for a while, or do I drop out of the race right then and there?

With God on board in our partnership, I usually get an urge for the change I need to make. I will follow that fresh thought and have faith in its outcome. As most of us know, sometimes there is not a sign of any sort. To me, that means He wants me to proceed with my thought pattern, as I need that personal challenge at that moment, regardless of the outcome. Since I understand that challenges lead to personal growth in some way, whether it's running or living moment-by-moment, I proceed with my running adjustment.

Worshiping

Many people in my local community would probably not characterize me as a quiet person. My past experiences here included 33 years of high school teaching and coaching, 20 years as a lead sportscaster and sports talk show host, 11 summer trips to Europe with students, five summer coaching trips to Hawaii with students, and seven winter and spring seasons of coaching Junior Olympic club sports. After retirement from all of that, I am still teaching, 15 years later, the Asian health and martial art of Tai Chi, and traveling: once to South Africa, and, to help complement my present teaching, four trips to mainland China, two trips to Taiwan, and one trip to Japan.

For sure, God has blessed me with unbelievable circumstances and the courage and guidance to pursue all of those opportunities! As a person who tries to stay and live in the moment and have awareness of what God has put around me each day, I often don't reflect on the past. Consequently, I don't thank God enough for my previous experiences. But I do now during my quiet moments, especially when I run.

Perhaps because of my previous busy lifestyle, and to some degree now, or merely because of my innate nature, I seek quiet moments whenever possible today. Running by myself is a choice. It allows me the opportunity to worship God and pray. My walking-jogging-running moments represent a spiritual time for me with God. It is He and I with the elements and conditions doing an activity together. At times, it seems like a continuous conversation, a private chat, or a soliloquy.

Sometimes, I simply listen to the peace and tranquility around me, as God speaks through His glorious nature. At other times, I worship and praise God with song. There are several I like from our church's repertoire, from which I will think, say, hum, or sing a line or two. Whether it's individual words, phrases, or complete lyrics, I feel a connection to God with some helpful meaning and motivation, especially at the end of a tiring run.

Thanking

My choices to run solo—and without any electronics for music or the monitoring of miles in different ways—are most likely not popular preferences for all the walkers and runners I see when I venture out into my neighborhoods. For now, I still consider myself a competitive runner, striving to "master" the circumstances as best I can and finish races as healthy and as efficiently as possible. Since each training run has some type of goal (i.e., speed, distance, elevation, weather acclimation, etc.), it is difficult to find even one other runner who has the same running ability and goals that I have on any given day. From my experiences in the past, I have found that partner or group running tends to compromise workout goals for everyone who still runs competitively.

A 12-minute miler, for example, needs to speed up his pace when running with a 10-minute miler. Similarly, the faster runner needs to slow down considerably, if he wants to run with the slower-paced mover. There are, of course, many programs and ideas available for any two runners to both get in a good workout, but their actual moments of running the same direction and at the same pace are minimal. The last time I tried to run and "keep up" with a faster partner, it only lasted about a mile, and it led to a hamstring pull for me that was still bothersome three weeks later at my next race.

By running alone, I can also put all my time into my personal goals. One hour of running and walking results in usually one hour of goal performance. With other runners, likely a portion of that hour would go towards the compromising necessary for multiple paces, etc. For me, the biggest advantage I like about solo running, is that I can have my personal, spiritual chats with God. Additionally, since I don't depend on electronic devices to run, I am able to put more focus on the running world around me and thank God for it. Because of this level of awareness, I am able to see and enjoy some of the most minute phenomena along the way, which generally, are helpful to me in some way. And I certainly let God know about it. Nearly every reference to Him starts with, *Thank You, God, for* . . . That applies also to any prayers at the beginning or end of a day, before meals, during devotions, or as necessary, during the course of any day.

Dear Heavenly Father, thank You for . . . or *Dear God, thank You for . . .* are my most common ways to get into communication mode with Him. Thanking comes first, and then, if necessary, additional thoughts or concerns come next.

God's Inspiration

It was mid-July 2019, and a few days after my return from one of my running highlights of the year. I had spent a substantial amount of time, thought, and physical, mental, and spiritual preparation for the challenging race and family get-together in Atlanta, Georgia. So, with the long drives, family times, and recent running efforts for that race behind me, the moment had come to decide what was next for me.

Certainly, I was going to keep up with my running training, at some level, since I had another race day coming. But I had three months for that preparation. But my biggest question was, *What should I do, if anything, about writing a potential book?* I had a few paragraphs written out and some notes that could be turned into manuscript form. With decent development of those, I might have eight to ten pages of copy? *Hmm . . . not exactly a book,* I thought!

Entering my mind were these questions, *Do I write this book, or not? If I write it, what level of excitement, enthusiasm, and dedication do I have for this project? Will I have enough content for this topic, or do I need to change my direction?* "God, I need Your help to figure all this out, especially since I want to put Your name in the title."

God answered me in a big way! He gave me content EVERY TIME I ran or walked! It was almost as if God was moving my pen for me. After I finished a run and returned home, I jotted down notes, as quick as I could, while they were still fresh in my mind. God blessed me with His guidance for this endeavor. He wanted me to do this book, and I decided to give it my best efforts. I still feel his presence. I am now not only running with God, but also writing with Him.

TRAINING WITH GOD | 4

Classic Neighborhood

Since I lived on McIntyre Drive, naturally, my initial running experience was in that neighborhood, about a mile and a half southeast of downtown Auburn. This avenue of passage was named after William McIntyre, one of several car-related names in the history of our town. For starters, the classic cars called the Auburns and the Cords were designed and manufactured here between the years of 1902 and 1936 by the Auburn Motor Company. This company also designed the classic muscle cars called the Duesenbergs in its administrative offices, which are today on display as part of the National Registry Auburn-Cord-Duesenberg Automobile Museum.

To add to this "classic" part of town are other manufactured-in-Auburn cars named after such notable personas as DeSoto, Kiblinger, and Zimmerman, who, like E. L. Cord, has a side street named after him. Each of these streets is within a two-block radius of McIntyre Drive. When I ran east on McIntyre, approximately one-third of a mile, I then came to the north-south Duesenberg Drive intersection. For a long time, this was my running world, surrounded by automobile history. Adding to the intrigue of this "car world" was the fact that the person who inspired me to take up running, Auburn resident Robert Sbarge, was the President and CEO of the Auburn Cord Duesenberg Automobile Museum! Synchronicity, perhaps? For me, it was simply, God seeing the big picture, as usual, and connecting and tying up multiple loose ends of life for the benefit of many.

Auburn Drive

Cathy had noticed that if I ran a little farther south on Duesenberg Drive, it came to a "T" at Auburn Drive. So, I followed her idea and ran to Auburn Drive. I had a choice to run left (east) or right (west). Since she had discovered the area and told me about the possibilities of going east with a sidewalk base, I took her suggestion. I turned left, stepped on the sidewalk, and said, "Good morning, God! I'm here and ready to run with you!" I had no idea where I was going. My level of faith cranked up a few notches right then. I knew there would be some sidewalk to keep me out of the street, but I didn't know how much.

Each running step added more depth to my faith. Each step was another one of trust, then confidence, then excitement. *Hmm . . . I wonder how far this fairly new paved sidewalk will go?* I noticed right away that the speed limit for cars and trucks was higher here on Auburn Drive than on the more residential Duesenberg Drive. *So nice to have that safe sidewalk,* I thought.

The more sidewalk, the less I would have to run on the asphalt of Auburn Drive.

The sidewalk and I both kept going east. I was gaining enthusiasm for what God had in store for me. After running past an open field on my left and about one-fifth of a mile from where I turned at the intersection, I began to notice some trees, also on my left (the north side of Auburn Drive). As I went further, I saw more trees, then a tree line that was running parallel to the sidewalk. Upon further investigation, I realized that this was a wooded area that had some depth, which I later determined to be at least a third of a mile. As I continued my running and looking, I noticed a deer stand in a tree, right at the edge of the woods. I couldn't believe it . . . sidewalk, nature, woods, and a hunter's perch. This was too good to be true, especially for a runner! Casting a glance to the southside of Auburn Drive, I saw more woods. This led me to believe that Auburn Drive was carved out from the center of a substantially thick woods, and its elevated sighting spot suggested where a deer run used to be? And the sidewalk indicated the beginnings of a future sub-division, perhaps?

I continued east and came to a point where the woods ended on my side of the street, but still extended eastwardly on the other side of Auburn Drive, perhaps another fifth of a mile. Both sides of the Drive displayed a lot of openness from that point on, with a large cornfield highlighting my left-hand side. This continued all the way to the intersection at County Road 35. All I could think and say was, *Thank You, God for this opportunity, this moment, these circumstances, AND this beauty!*

Still today, this is where the sidewalk ends, approximately eight-tenths of a mile from the Duesenberg Drive intersection. For some, this distance may not sound like much, but each running venture gives me a minimum of 1.6 miles with a round trip. What a blessing to have that distance with safe passage!

From that moment on, running has been and still is a spiritual adventure for me. Every walk, jog, run, or "sprint," whether in training or in a race, is spiritually-based now. I totally enjoy my personal runs and talks with God. I feel that He wants me to experience Him and His works, to use my senses as I run, and see along the way all the beauty there is in His world. With God, sidewalk, and nature, I was ready to restart my running career.

In the Beginning

In trying to find my niche and comfort in the world of running, I tried a number of "staying in the moment" mindsets and motivations to help me log miles that were safe and healthy. One of these was to simply count the cars and other vehicles that passed by me from either direction, as I ran along Auburn Drive. Of course, in the early stages of building up my distances per run, the number of vehicles I saw was understandably low compared to longer runs, later in my career. I was excited on days when I counted a total of 50 cars and other vehicles, which was a milestone for me to measure endurance development.

Over the history of my running career, now totaling 15 years, almost all my runs have been in the morning, as early as possible, to not interfere with each day's main commitments. As time went on with my morning miles, I learned quickly that getting to the count of 50 came much sooner on a weekday than on a Sunday. (I rarely ran on a Saturday morning, unless it was a race day.) So, eventually, on a weekday morning run during "rush hour" on a "secondary" road, I was happy when the count hit 100, and when it totaled 150, I stopped counting. That meant, it was a remarkably busy morning drive for many or I had run, generally, for about an hour and a half.

Even though every day can be considered a God day, certainly Sunday the Sabbath has some reverence for me. The early morning traffic on that day is always far less than on any weekday that I have run. I assume that more people in our local neighborhoods are off from work and are perhaps sleeping in a bit later. With that premise, I look forward to the increased number of vehicles as the morning progresses, and optimistically I hope that as many as possible are heading to one of God's churches. My thoughts include, *God, show them the way to one of Your special places and give them safe travel this morning.* I have no idea how many vehicles pursued that notion or mini-prayer, but I try to put that thought and energy out there and hope that maybe a few extras might find their way to a Sunday gathering. For those keeping count, I rarely saw 150 vehicles on a Sunday morning run, hopefully, for two good reasons. One is that my runs got done sooner than they used to (so I could get to church), and perhaps secondly, a substantial number of people were at church in the mid-to-late morning!

Metal and Iron Friends

In the early stages of training on Auburn Drive where there were no houses going up, I noticed other aspects of life, such as the vehicles coming from both the east and west. Little did their drivers know that I appreciated every one of them. I was happy that God had given them good enough health to be driving. Also, especially on the warmer days, I appreciated the extra breeze they gave me to help keep me cooled off. And on the very hot days, it was, *Thank You, God, for those large trucks You sent my way!* I especially liked the dump trucks, cement mixers, and the big rig semis, all of which almost always "packed a punch" of refreshing air! Occasionally, my baseball cap or visor got knocked off my head due to those oncoming breezes. It was exciting and exhilarating mostly, except when I was doing a timed run, and I had to retrace my steps and retrieve my head and sun protector!

The "little guys," the cars, gave me a helpful boost as well, especially when one was a mile or two over the posted speed. If a breeze came from behind, I was thankful for the extra boost I received. To me, it was a little extra "push" from God's hand to assist me. If the added breeze came at me, I was thankful for the refreshment to keep me cooled down, especially on a high sweat run. Either way, I still appreciate today God's partnership with my running and thank Him for giving me what I need, whenever I need it for each day's journey.

Other metal "friends" along the way are at my feet. They are the standard and round iron sewer covers. While a couple of them are on the land side of the sidewalk where I run, the others are located on the concrete itself, close to the land. Some of the tops of these iron circles are basically flat, and others are perforated with half-inch blunted "spikes." It appears they are functionally spaced, generally, every 100 feet or so. Depending on my stride at the moment, I can step on up to 20 of these helpful aides on one eastward pass along Auburn Drive.

As I run, especially after a quantity of miles, I try to land on them purposely, without breaking stride. Even though it is of minimal value, if at all, I consider the contact, especially on the perforated ones, as a brief foot massage, that can also reflect positively to other parts of the body. I take the same approach when I cross an intersection, trying to land on the hard rubber bumpy pad located on the declined curbs at both ends of the pedestrian crosswalk. Even if these special steps do nothing for me physically, at least mentally, I get a positive "perk" for my run.

Driver Courtesy

On a personal level, I notice and appreciate the courtesies extended to me by the drivers. When I run westward on Auburn Drive, there are intersections for me to cross at Duesenberg Drive, County Road 46A, and County Road 29. Each is considered a fairly busy artery for the south side of our city. Even though, by law, as soon as I enter the crosswalk zone, I have the right of way, as a runner, I rarely take advantage of that. To me, any space that is not on the sidewalk or curb belongs to the vehicles.

My goal is to not interrupt a vehicle from negotiating an intersection as efficiently as possible. In nearly all cases, I'm sure, their destination on a given day is probably farther away than mine is. If both the vehicle and I can get through an intersection without either of us adjusting to the other, then we collectively have "mastered" that moment. If I sense that our speeds could cause us a possible impact on the crosswalk, then I'll stay at the curb and "run in place" until the traffic clears. Because of so many caring and courteous drivers, I rarely, maybe only a handful of times a year, need to use that option.

Surprisingly, many drivers could easily get to the intersection with their normal speed, make their stop, and proceed to turn or go straight, before I get to the crosswalk. Instead, many choose to go well beyond an accepted level of being cautious and courteous, and they stop and wait for me to not only get to the pedestrian lane, but also for me to get to the curb on the other side. *God bless them, for allowing a runner to keep his stride!* I respond to them with a wave of my hand and then display a thumbs-up. *God, thank You so much,* I reflect. If you think their kindness is at a high level, it is even more so in the late fall, winter, and early spring, when I'm sure, some added sympathy factors in. Drivers probably detect and observe, with accuracy, that I am cold, old, and slow! I am so grateful that we can share space harmoniously, all as "children of God," as referenced often in Scripture and song.

Running Reality

Since I started my running career a little later in life than any of my local running "friends," achieving significantly fast race times is definitely not my goal. Likely, from a physical perspective, it will not ever happen. My first 10K race took me over 68 minutes for the 6.2 miles. The winning time that day was an astounding 27 minutes and a few seconds! *Wow,* I thought, *that's six miles of high-level sprinting for me, with each mile run at approximately 4.5 minutes!* By starting my racing career at the age of 56, that kind of time is not even close to realistic for me, at least not in this lifetime, with this body, and with this pair of legs! But I had faith and confidence that God's plan for my running journey was going to accomplish many other goals and unique experiences, as long as I ran with Him and followed His lead.

Running solo allows me to spend undivided time with God. I am able to be open to what I experience and what urgings are forthcoming. This brings calmness, awareness, and peace of mind to my journey. In his book, *Walking with God: How to Hear His Voice,* John Eldredge states, *"Whatever our situ-*

ation in life . . . our deepest and most pressing need is to learn to walk with God. To hear his voice. To follow him intimately."

Looking for One

Since I like to run year-round and outdoors as much as possible, my running gear—including hydration and nutrition needs, warm clothing, foot and head coverings, and sunglasses—is extremely important to me. None are at the upper level of expensive, but they are items that make my runs more comfortable, enjoyable, and bearable.

One day I did a seven-mile run, targeting distance rather than speed. The run began in sunlight and ended in much cloudiness. Not needing my sunglasses at some point, I affixed them to my water belt behind my lower back. When I finished my run and returned home, I noticed one of the plastic lenses was missing. *Oh, boy, what do I do now?* I definitely need sunglasses for running and other outside activities. *Do I consider it a loss and simply spend $10–15 on another pair, or do I go after that lens piece and retrace the approximate final five miles of my course, when cloudiness emerged?*

Cathy shared her perspective about the potential time it could take while looking for it, as well as the possible negative end result of not finding it. For me, it was a reminder of a parable that I've heard often at our church, as well as in some of our related songs. That is, how important it was for God's Son, Jesus, to go after the one lost sheep, while leaving the other ninety-nine. I valued each of my items that helped me run healthy and successfully, so I went after the inexpensive small piece of plastic. Since my decision was made rather quickly, I sensed that God not only wanted me to have that experience, but He also planned to help me through it, which He did.

Yes, I found my "lost sheep." This small, dark green, plastic item was camouflaged among dozens of similar-sized and larger black clumps of asphalt that had been splattered and hardened during the last repaving of that section of Auburn Drive. These dark spots "peppered" the sidewalk for a distance of about a third of a mile, and my little piece of plastic laid among them.

I found it a little more than a mile from our house. It was still in one piece, and I continued using it. I returned home in less than 30 minutes. Looking back on that situation, it probably wasn't a decision that most people would make, but when clarity to pursue this came so fast, I knew I had to do it, and I'm glad I did.

Signage

Over the stretch of nearly two miles of Auburn Drive that I run frequently, a number of road signs hang on posts. These are informational by nature and designed for the motorists. However, God knows that these are blessings for me too. I depend on them, especially the two that mark the beginning and end of my personal Auburn Drive trek.

On the northwest corner where Auburn Drive and County Road 35 connect, I tap the stop sign. This light contact symbolizes for me the accomplishment of finishing today's eastward journey. *Thank You, God, for bringing me safely to that end.* While still moving, I turn around and head to the west. Immediately, I notice the difference in wind velocity, either gaining today's wind at my back or "enjoying" a breeze in my face. Regardless of the wind intensity, such as a gentle breeze of a few miles per hour or a much more challenging gust of 20 to 30 miles per hour, I appreciate what I've got for the moment. *Thank You, God, for this variable, as I know it is the climate circumstance I need at this moment, and You have met my need!*

Similarly, when I reach my westward destination, there is another informational sign for me to tap before turning around and heading back east. *Are these sign taps necessary for my runs?* Probably not. But they are little motivators to help me on my day's journey. Actually, this west sign is located about two normal running strides beyond the end of the sidewalk. So, briefly, I get to travel on a small parcel of land that reminds me of the common phrase, "God's green earth."

Like "baby steps" in the process of growing up, touching a sign is, for me, accomplishing one of my steps for that day's journey. This idea of touching a sign as a symbolic gesture of a small accomplishment came to me from the character, Rocky, after one of his daily runs that took him up the rather steep and infamous stairs in Philadelphia during the *Rocky* movies.

> "It's the little details that are vital.
> Little things make big things happen."
> JOHN WOODEN, American Basketball Coach

On two other courses, where I run, there are painted arrows on the pathways. They are leftovers from previous races that were run at those locations. They are directional in nature to ensure that walkers, runners, and bikers in competition stay on their respective courses. Even though this signage is at my feet, there is still meaning for me, as I see these arrows as God's message to me to keep going and stay the course that He has planned for me. *Thank You, God, for helping me see the beauty and meaning in everything, even if it is simply a sign or an arrow.*

HELPING GOD'S COMMUNITY

5

Precious Blood

Before I could get married in the early 1970s, it was a requirement to have a blood test soon before the important event. It's normally a quick procedure with hardly any blood taken. However, it was my first time for any kind of blood draw, and anxiety overcame me. Embarrassment came next, as I passed out right in front of my fiancée and woke up with my head between my knees! She still married me, but I vowed to never do a blood draw again.

About 15 years later, my good friend George, whom I met through our church Sunday school class, was battling Hodgkin's disease and needed blood for a vitally important procedure. I thought, *Yikes, what do I do now?* This would be a normal draw of a full pint! I prayed, "God, I *have* to do this for my friend. Please help me get through it." He did. It wasn't the smoothest procedure; I sweated significantly out of anxiety; I didn't pass out; and I donated my first pint ever! *Praise God!*

After that episode, out of thankfulness to God and dedication to my friend, who passed away soon thereafter, I decided to donate blood once a year. During the summers worked best for me, since I had more time available from my school responsibilities. Later in life, when I retired from the school system, I began donating multiple times each year. Thanks to God's presence and my friend, this non-donor has become a regular Red Cross contributor who surpassed the ten-gallon donation mark a couple years ago.

God has helped me come "full circle" in this category of my life, and I am forever thankful. My highest level of disappointment these days is when I show up for a blood donation, and I'm not able to proceed because my iron level is not at the Red Cross standards. Those occasional moments are usually in the summer, when, according to the nurses, I've sweated away some of my iron content due to my running workouts. It simply means that my intake of iron-rich foods needs to be better balanced.

Silent Prayer

Whenever I am out driving my car and see another vehicle experiencing what appears to be an unfortunate situation, at the minimum I wish the best for them through silent prayer. If, for some reason, I am not able to help right away, I pray to God for His assistance. Even if a car and its occupants appear to be safely on the side of the road and their help has already arrived, I still say a short prayer from the wheel of my car, "God, please help them with whatever needs they have at this moment." If there is no traffic to the front, sides, or back of my moving car, I will close my eyes for a quick second to help make my prayer personal.

If my circumstances do not allow me to safely assist another person at that moment, I always feel confident that God has a plan for that situation and will take care of matters as timely and efficiently as He sees fit. *Do your best, and let God do the rest.* Sometimes a prayer is my best assistance, and I trust God will finish off the request.

Good Neighbor

At the combined age of 127 and counting, Cathy and I made a conscientious decision to begin downsizing our quantities of nearly everything we owned. As "empty-nesters," we had considerable extra space on our property that wasn't being used routinely. Also, we wanted to have more time for grandkids in exchange for that time that used to go towards yardwork and other household maintenance concerns. In summary, we were blessed with the opportunity to cut back on our house space by 800 square feet, our property size overall, our unnecessary clothes and other items. We eliminated lawnmowing, leaf-raking, and snow-shoveling from our agendas by moving into a villa that is part of a duplex. We still live totally independent with our own residence, driveway, and yard, but each is considerably smaller than before. Additionally, we have new neighbors, who are only a few feet away, actually, on the other side of a wall.

The married couple "on the other side" goes by the names

of Glenn and Kay. The neighborly, positive chemistry among the four of us has been so surprisingly incredible that Cathy and I consider this happenstance a godsend. The age difference between the two wives is a scant three years, and both ladies have lived all, or most of their lives, here in Auburn. Also, both have spent a great deal of their professional careers serving at area hospitals.

For Glenn and me, our age difference is only one and a half years. Both of us have had some teaching experience, as well as some additional employment opportunities on the side. We both enjoy the many benefits that our local YMCA offers, and we drive there together three times a week to do our workouts. He is also a man of faith, and we both have recently launched our first professional attempt in the creative arts. His was a production of a CD of Christian music entitled, "The Bridges We Cross," and mine was the aforementioned book.

As an added bonus to me, Glenn's friendship and numerous conversations have given me an "open forum"—in addition to Cathy—for some faith-based discussions. Throughout my professional career as a teacher, coach, and communications employee, expressions of personal preference with regard to subjects like politics and religion were not suitable in those public arenas. With our common faith beliefs in God, it is refreshing for me to have the time and opportunity for meaningful discussions so close to home! "Thank You, God, for the direction You have shown us in making our lifestyle transition, as we have moved forward with the aging process and for the immediate next-door neighbors You have placed beside us to complement our journey in faith with You. We ask for Your continued guidance so that we can be of best service to them to meet Your and their needs."

God's Givers

An annual summer event in our local DeKalb County is "Day of Caring." Dozens of individuals and several groups sign up to volunteer their skills for a few hours. On the flip side are the needs that individuals and groups have indicated, where they could use some assistance with yard projects or repairs. Overseers of the various projects then match the two sides together for a unified caring and sharing that significantly enhances many properties around the county.

When I arrived at the local YMCA on the morning of July 26, 2019, the Day of Caring was already in full swing. Several volunteers were trimming and raking around shrubbery and preparing to plant some small fir trees around the periphery of the facility. On that day I chose to run on the YMCA-owned pathway located about two-tenths of a mile to the north of the premises. This continuous path encircles seven full-sized soccer fields in the YMCA Sports Complex at James Park.

As I began my running on this hot, humid morning, I noticed perhaps 30 young spruce trees, ready for planting, being dropped off strategically throughout the complex. As I continued my running, I noticed volunteers arriving at those tree locations, preparing to dig holes and set the young firs in their designated places. My first thought was, *Thank You, God, for bringing these beautiful spruce trees and volunteers to the same area where I am today.* It was inspiring to me to watch the effort and energy, combined with the positive individual and group spirit of these volunteers, working on that sweat-inducing day. They were clearly working for God, and each was graciously donating his time.

On one section of the path, spruces were going up on both sides of me. One of the workers asked me as I passed by, "How far is it around these fields?" I said, "A little less than a mile." He responded, "Keep going, you inspire me!" *Whoa, hit the pause button!* While I looked forward to seeing them each time around the course and was so grateful for their presence and inspiration, I had not realized that they were also looking forward to my appearance with each lap. *Was it because I was also sweating due to a different type of effort and I appeared to be about 30 or 35 years older than they were?* I'll never know why, but in God's way He was evidently using me to be a mode of encouragement and inspiration for them to maintain their focus and keep going too, especially with the warm conditions! Because of this realization and God's urging, I ran two laps more than I planned and waved at those dedicated volunteers each time I passed.

God's Builders

As I ran my Auburn Drive course, east of the Duesenberg Drive intersection, I enjoyed watching a new street and houses developing. It was encouraging to observe a positive housing industry thriving in our neighborhood and to see the construction frames looking more "house-like" each time I ran by. When workers were on large and potentially dangerous equipment or putting rafters up, I asked God for their safety.

Sometimes, before I turned the corner to run east on Auburn Drive, I guessed where the progress might be with one of the houses. *Where on the property are the workers today?* I listened for sounds to give me a clue, such as from a hammer, power nail gun or saw, cement mixer, or even workers chattering or giving directions as they unified their efforts on a project area. Collectively, they were God's workers doing His work.

Seeing that one street "community" evolve from open fields to houses on both sides of the street—with developed yards, concrete driveways and sidewalks, and eventually home-owners and family units—was inspiring! God's hand-iwork of taking His servants to create—not only employment and livelihood for some but also family unity and community for others—was truly an example of the ultimate Master at work. The result was the Oak Chase cul-de-sac with 15 new residences.

God's Work

A few thoughts, mottos, philosophies that I like in my life, include: *Live in the moment*; *Focus on the moment*; *Be aware of your surroundings*; *Enjoy the beauty of God's work all around*; and *Be open to and appreciate change.* No change on Auburn Drive was more physically, mentally, and spiritually noticeable, heart-warming, and uplifting than the new Auburn Baptist Church erected on the northeast corner of the intersection of County Road 46A (Old Brick Road) and Auburn Drive.

I ran a training session or drove my car past that site al-most daily during the summer and fall months of 2016. If my scheduled run on a particular day kept me a little east of that intersection, I added an extra tenth of a mile or two in order to see the most recent progress. Each time, I marveled at what had been visibly completed since my last run in that area.

I was motivated by the initial group of builders, many of whom had come from other states in mid-June. In God's spirit of doing something to help others, it was clearly evident that these "worker-bees" were passionate about serving one of God's many missions around the country. A majority of the first workers, those who put up the exterior framework, walls, and roof of the large structure, had travelled quite a distance north, representing an organization called Men on Mission from Trussville, Alabama. Others from the 99-man construction crew came from the states of Vermont, Delaware, Pennsylvania, South Carolina, and Missouri. The fact that nearly ninety percent of the workers were not professional carpenters also impressed me.

These volunteers were on a one-week mission trip and were energetically active on the premises, basically from sun-up to sun-down. Watching the unified group of workers blend in for a common cause was inspiring to me. Seeing the out-of-town vehicles parked by the worksite reminded me of the "brotherhood" God would like all of us to exhibit regularly. When I ran by, I prayed for appropriate weather, safe work, and God's guiding hand to take the project from an open field to the topmost part of the steeple. This unity and spirit of volunteerism reminded me of a scene from one of my favorite Hollywood movies, *Witness.* In it, actor Harrison Ford's character and a throng of God-spirited Amish community-dwellers erected an enormous pole barn with walls, roof, and side panels, for a neighbor, in only one day!

> *"Let us think of ways to motivate one another
> to acts of love and good works."*
> HEBREWS 10:24

Cemetery Respect

On another fall run, I passed the Woodlawn Cemetery (northwest corner of the intersection of Auburn Drive and County

Road 29). I made eye contact with the superintendent, who was aboard his riding mower. Since he was facing me, I gave him a quick wave. Later, after I finished my run to my western point and headed back east, I came to the cemetery again. While I had run about a half mile, he had mowed several strips of that special property and was facing me again. This time he was only a few feet away. As he finished up another mower-width strip, which abutted the sidewalk on which I was running, he was reversing his machine to begin his next strip of land, when our eyes met. I gave him a thumbs-up as my appreciation for his dedication and the work he had done.

Even though he didn't know me, someday, he will be my earthly caretaker. Cathy and I have reserved one of those cherished plots, which awaits our arrival in some form, when the time comes. He responded with a smile and a nod. My silent wish was that his apparent good health continues and that he still enjoys his work when he becomes our caretaker. Maybe today's greetings and thoughts will help make that happen? My guess is, with that line of work, as overseer of the entire cemetery, life and work there can get a little lonely and underappreciated at times.

UNDERSTANDING GOD'S MOMENTS

6

God is #1 Boss

Whether I am working for a boss or for other people, God is my overall boss. He wants me to directly or indirectly affect others in a positive way. Work for Him at all times was the pastor's themed message a few years ago at our local church. This mindset can be calming and nurturing for any worker, especially where there might be tensions in the employer-employee relationship.

I have "run" with this concept for a long time. My goal on a daily basis is to do my best efforts at work, and elsewhere, for God and let Him take care of the rest of what He feels is necessary for His people and His world. Since the word "best" is a superlative, there is nothing better than a person's best. I sense that if something can be done at a higher level than my circumstances and abilities allow at that moment, then God will show me the way to make improvements or refinements going forward. "Do your best, and let God do the rest," is one of my personal mottos.

To God, there are no incidental jobs. Every job, large or small, dirty or clean, has purpose and importance to His world of people. Every job affects or helps somebody, somehow. If for no other reason, a job that earns income gives an employee spending ability to purchase various needs and wants for him and family members. And purchases help businesses and the economy.

If someone is doing a volunteer assignment without a wage, he is rewarded internally with an uplifted spirit and the knowledge that most likely his performance has helped others either physically, mentally, spiritually, or in some other way. Consider putting God at the forefront of your next required assignment and see what happens to you and your productivity. Choose God as your boss and simply "run" with it! And maybe words like "work" and "task" may not be common vocabulary for you in the future.

> *"Work with enthusiasm,*
> *as though you were working for the Lord*
> *rather than for people."*
> EPHESIANS 6:7

Personal Growth

Running with God makes me mindful of what He has created in His world and what small part I play in it. With awareness and mindfulness, it is truly inspirational to me what people I meet, what things I feel, what sounds I hear, what creatures

I see, what songs I sing, and what mottos I say. Without His presence on this phase of my journey through life, I am certain I would have missed out on a great deal of life's experiences.

I view any variable or circumstance that comes my way as a detail of life, what I need at that moment in time. I see these challenges, and how I choose to deal with them, as opportunities for personal growth. Running up a steep hill and against a stiff breeze may not be a fun moment, but I have learned to embrace those temporary challenges as part of the learning curve of life, in general, and also for my running. I thank God for these moments of opportunity and continue to look forward to what He has in store for me going forward.

At church on Sunday, August 4, a part of the pastoral message was that God sets us up with challenges. Even though I have known and experienced that for a long time, it was encouraging to have my thoughts on that topic confirmed. As I run, challenges come moment-by-moment, sometimes second-by-second. I am constantly assessing my circumstances with regard to weather conditions, the terrain, creatures large and small nearby, and, of course, all the many body parts involved that "tweak" or "squawk" their displeasure when certain conditions arise.

I feel that God always gives me what I need. It is then my challenge to assess the ever-changing variables, make adjustments if possible, and then "master" those moments to the best of my ability with God's help. While running, making changes to my posture, tempo, or stride are but a few of the changes necessary. In both running and non-running activities throughout any day, living in and focusing on the moments of life have become routine goals. These concepts became the central theme of my aforementioned first book.

Faith or Logic

That early August church message also challenged us to find the appropriate middle ground between faith and logic. Only three days later I got to experience what that concept was all about. On that Wednesday I explored an opportunity to teach Tai Chi at another location. Ironically, within the previous three or four days I had been contemplating what the scenario could be for me to at least consider dropping off the teaching of some of my classes.

I was already teaching at four different locations on four days a week. At three sites, my instruction was once weekly. At the other, which is the main hub of our school, I taught six classes per week. In addition to being the Head Instructor and overseer of the school, I had all the documental and financial responsibilities of the school, while serving the secretary and treasurer positions as well.

I was probably doing a bit too much considering I had already "retired" from my third-of-a-century professional career of high school teaching and coaching. That "retirement" lasted only one month! In addition, our growing family had seen the birth of five grandkids in the past four and a half years, bringing the present total to six. Not to mention that only half of them live in-state now. I will also complete another decade of living when I celebrate my next birthday. So those variables had recently started me to at least ponder what retirement number two might look like, not only for me, but also for our school and family life.

Meanwhile, an independent living facility for the senior-aged population had recently opened up and was trying to secure appropriate and healthy activities for its residents. They contacted me and requested that I come for a visit. I thought, *What, really God! Now?* For many years I had hoped for an opportunity to expand our classes to the much larger community to our immediate south. This was the substantially large city of Fort Wayne, the second largest in the state of Indiana. My second thought was, *God, is this legitimate, or are You only "messing" with me?*

On the day before I travelled to the facility, I told Cathy that logic certainly dictated that this is not a situation that would normally exist or one in which I could be successful. Looking to start a new adventure at my age, when I already had a fairly crowded schedule of activities and obligations for each day of the week, didn't make any logical sense.

Since the logic versus faith topic was recently fresh in our minds, I discussed with her that this decision to explore this possibility was definitely faith-based and God-driven. With good logic she reminded me that it is my desire to be "totally" retired from teaching at some point in life. My initial 33-year teaching career has simply led to another 15-year teaching career and still counting! I told her that I thought God wanted me to do this for some reason. I agreed with her that it didn't make logical sense, but spiritually I felt the need to at least explore this, especially if it is God's direction for me to share my experiences in this area.

I concluded that what God had in store for me would be revealed soon. If it was His will for me to interact with and meet some new people and share my experiences with them pertaining to this healthy subject matter, then so be it. Working for Him with His people has been a core principle of mine for a long time. I'll "run" with God and pursue it to the best of my ability. *Do my best, and let God do the rest.*

After the interview in Fort Wayne, which led to a new teaching opportunity for me, I returned to our local YMCA facility in Auburn to pick-up my neighbor friend Glenn, whom I had dropped off on my way to the interview. Since all variables went smoothly for me in the big city, I had a little extra time at the Y, while he finished his workout. I waited a few minutes close to the entry door, in case he might have finished early.

Then I thought, *I might as well do something here at the Y, even though I still have on my "business casual" street clothes.* I only needed a few minutes to do a quick set of exercises on a weight machine or two. The biceps curl and triceps extension machines, which are both merely a few walking strides from the door, came to mind. I figured I could do a few reps and still get back into the hallway, so he would see me when he came. I thought, *Alright, it's doable. Let's go for it!* So, I opened the door to the Fitness Center, and before I took the first step in, I sensed an urging to take one more look down the hallway. Sure enough, he had come out of the locker room and was heading toward me!

Admittedly, at that moment, I was a little disappointed, because I was motivated to accomplish something at the Y today, since I had given up my normal fitness plan to make the trip to Fort Wayne. So, I did not enter the room, met my friend, and proceeded homeward. Not until later in the day did I realize that if I had I done those arm exercises, I might have done something severely dangerous to myself. Because my focus had been on that interview in Fort Wayne, I had completely forgotten that I had donated blood to the American Red Cross the previous afternoon. Since this was the next morning, I had definitely not followed the nurse's final urgent words of caution: "No heavy lifting for at least 24 hours!" Yikes, that was a close call! God's urging for me to take one final look down the hallway was as timely as possible. God knew what was best for me!

"I am the Lord your God, who teaches you what is good for you and leads you along the paths you should follow."

ISAIAH 48:17

Winter Blessings

Winters in northeastern Indiana can and usually do bring a myriad of outside weather elements. Extreme cold temperatures with wind chill can be minus 30 to 50 degrees Fahrenheit. We usually get our fair share of ice and snow, as well as sleet and freezing rain. I try to run outside as often as it is reasonable for me, without treading on dangerous footing. Especially if we have a day with sunshine, I run outside unless it is too cold for me. Usually my cut-off is the plus 18- to 20-degree range. I am blessed to have sidewalks in neighboring sub-divisions and, of course, on my favorite route, Auburn Drive. If there is only snow on the sidewalks, and it is not piled too high, I can run safely there. If there is ice on the sidewalks but it has receded some so that I still have basically half of the walkway clear, it's a "green light" for me to still run on that surface. Too much ice or snow, or ice under snow are hazards that I definitely avoid. Even though I have to take some of my running indoors during the winter months, I greatly treasure those outdoor runs in "wonderlands of beauty" that God has created and given to all of us to enjoy. Running with God through snow-covered tree areas on both sides of me, with sidewalk under each step, is winter and spiritual bliss!

Best Laid Plans . . .

Since I had run my "distance day" on a Wednesday this particular week, instead of the normal Tuesday, I decided to "tame down" my Friday workout to a walking routine outside. This would give me more time, then, to do some of the weight machines in the YMCA Fitness Center, before going to my Friday morning yoga class. Because the Friday morning Holy Yoga instructor, Randi, likes to emphasize several upper-body stretches for strength, such as planks, I decided to do the machines that focused on the middle and lower body regions. So, after a long distance run only two days previous, I felt I had the right mix of activities lined up for the day. Ha! What's that quote that goes something like, "Man plans, God laughs!"?

So, the first change of plans came as I was making the transition from walking a couple miles outside to entering the Y to do some machine work. As I walked to my car in the parking lot, one of God's "messengers," a runner whom I had seen often recently, came over to me and started up a conversation. I did not know him, but I sensed immediately that I was in the right place at the right time. God had a purpose for our intersection that day.

He introduced himself as Mo and began to tell me his story about how he got into running. There was both humbleness and pride at the same time for this middle-aged man. He had made some poor choices earlier in life that took his health to an unusually low level. And today, with those vices behind him, he now runs about 20 or 25 miles per week and in several local races. *What an inspiring story he told me!*

After that, he inquired about my start to running. I told him that my inspiration came from my Tai Chi master, who

Following God's paths around every turn at YMCA complex in early spring

Running with nature on Auburn Drive in winter

Summer run on East Auburn Drive, 2016

Thousands of miles of journeys with God

*Brothers and "sisters" celebrating Peachtree Race
and Independence Day in Atlanta, Georgia, 2018*

*Wife, Cathy, and Author (top) overseeing God's
children at family Christmas, 2019*

was not only my mentor for that Asian health and martial art, but also an avid distance runner. Since I run and teach now on a regular basis, Mo indicated his interest in my backstory.

There was no question God had sent him, so we could meet and chat in the parking lot. Our paths had crossed a couple times previously on runs around the Y facility or the soccer fields to the north. But, each time, we were both in running mode and going in opposite directions when we passed. At the end of our conversation, he started another run, while I headed into the Y.

Even though I had used up my allotted time for the Fitness Center, I was thankful for that unexpected occurrence in the parking lot. I treasured that godsend happening then and still do today, as a total stranger shared so much of his past and present circumstances in a calm and confident manner. God placed another amazingly influential person on my trail of life. I was honored to be there for a fellow runner.

Inside the Y, I headed straight to the Friday morning Holy Yoga class. There I noticed my second unexpected surprise of the day. The normal instructor Randi was not available to teach, and one of her associates was in charge of the class. From my experiences, I've learned that every instructor has his or her own points of emphasis. Even though I was expecting a different leader that day, our substitute April was obviously inspired by God and led class with a true spiritual passion. Through God's Holy Spirit, she gave me the yoga session that I needed the most to help me enhance my goal of mind-body-spirit balance. On the way out of class, I wanted to thank her in some way that conveyed my total appreciation for her heartfelt efforts. I shared a biblical reference and said, "Thank you, and well done, good servant!" This seemed to be an inspirational, emotional trigger for her.

It was only 11 a.m. on a Friday morning, and I had already been blessed beyond belief by God in so many ways! Two total strangers entered my life today and shared their inner essence, time, and talents with me. *Thank You, God, for the messengers You continue to send me and for the inspiration they give me.*

SEEING GOD'S MESSENGERS

7

Once Is Enough

I truly do appreciate each person I encounter on the sidewalk areas of Auburn Drive. I sense each has been sent by God as a messenger to assist me in some way. Whether it is a racer, runner, jogger, walker, dog walker, infant stroller pusher, or biker, I look forward to those moments of sharing "God's space."

It is especially rewarding when our immediate destinations are in opposite directions: we share a few brief moments and our eyes meet. My way of thanking God and them for their collective presence on the course is to acknowledge their efforts in some way. To those who are running, I will usually give them a wave with my hand that is closer to them, especially if they are wearing earplugs and perhaps, listening to music. To those in "walk mode," I acknowledge them verbally with "Good morning," "Have a nice day," or, "Have a nice walk." Almost always, my verbal cues draw an oral response, generally with "Thanks!" or "You too!"

On one early summer occasion in June 2019, I encountered a middle-aged couple enjoying a casual Sunday stroll. As I approached them and our eyes met, I said, "Have a nice walk!" The response back to me from the gentleman was "Have a nice trot!" *Trot! Did I hear him correctly?* Overreacting to most matters in life, generally, is not my "cup of tea." But trotting— yikes! At least, I was jogging or running at a decent pace for me. To him, I guess, what I was doing was trotting or he didn't understand the world of running.

In all my interactions with people during training and being among thousands of participants and spectators on race days, I had *never* heard the word "trot" mentioned in any context! To me, that would be like calling a racehorse a burro, or a sprinter a turtle! Normally, I run four to six races competitively every year and over 700 miles total—and I'm a trotter! I have seen some beautiful trotting by horses in showmanship competition, but for me, as a runner, it is only one small level above "running in place," not getting too far, too fast.

God, help me to understand that his true intention was not a spiteful remark, and show me how to best use what I perceived initially as a negative into some kind of a positive going forward. I totally appreciate all the good will that has come from others regarding my running experiences, but I definitely prefer not hearing the word "trot" again in reference to my running journey.

That sidewalk episode still lingers with me today, and I am happy to say on behalf of all runners that I've been around since that moment, I have not heard that word again. Today, when someone approaches, I try to be in some other movement mode rather than "trotting." Perhaps, someday if or when my running career takes a different direction and "trotting" is my top speed, it will be a compliment. Time will tell. Only God knows, and if it happens, He will be there to help.

Strangers in Need

Later in June on a Sunday morning, I was near the end of my walking warm-up before I started my run. I was in the Mason's Village subdivision, approaching the intersection "T" of Auburn Drive, where I would start my run. Only about eight houses away and around the corner from the "T" I noticed a much younger man, perhaps in his early twenties. We were walking opposite directions, he on the sidewalk and I on the street. My pace had picked up, as I prepared to start my run in about a minute, and his gait had a noticeable limp. At 7 a.m. on a silent Sunday morning with no people, dogs, or cars on the street yet and all garage doors closed, something didn't seem right.

Of course, it's "normal" for a "crazy" runner to be the only one out on the streets at this time, but the other guy? *Hmm.* Our eyes met, and I noticed some degree of concern on his face. So I said, "Good morning! Have a good day!" He stopped, and responded with, "Do you live around here?" *Hmm, again.* He added, "I didn't want to knock on doors or ring doorbells. Do you have a "splash" of gas? I just need a little—to get me to the gas station. I can gather a few coins around." I said, "Not necessary. I have some gas in a can at home, but I don't know how much. I can run back home, grab the can, and be back in ten to fifteen minutes." He said, "God bless you!" and that he would wait on Auburn Drive, where the car was stranded.

Without seeing the car and with total faith in God that He placed me in this situation for a reason, I started my morning run, not on Auburn Drive as planned, but towards my house, a good half mile away. Of course, many thoughts entered my mind about how this scenario might play out. One thought was the visual of me running, probably a little faster than usual, holding a one-gallon gas can! I was willing and prepared to do that until right before approaching our house. Then a thought struck me, that I could get the necessary gas back to the stranded guy and car more quickly if I drove my car to the scene.

I was so pleased that I had at least a small amount of gas in my can, actually about a third of a gallon. After a quick briefing to Cathy for the reason why I wasn't running then and where I was taking our car, I headed to the place where there was supposedly a stranded car. Upon my arrival, I saw not only the car and the guy, but also another guy who came out of the driver's seat. He appeared to be a couple years older than the first guy, didn't say much, and was apparently the owner of the car.

If this were a Hollywood movie script and ominous music started, I would add truthfully that the second guy seemed to favor the color black. The body of his car and its interior and tires, as well as his wearing apparel were all sporting that color. From my martial arts training, my awareness level of these surroundings became more acute. If this whole scenario was a hoax, I was at that moment out-numbered. I truly didn't think of any negatives, however, sensing simply that God had a mission for me to help them.

The car's owner didn't say anything, poured in all the gasoline, and tried to start the car. Nope, it wasn't happening. That extremely empty gas tank needed more fuel. At that point, I was happy that I had brought my car. *A God urging, no doubt!* I said, "I'll take you to the gas station (a little over a mile away) and we'll get more. Do you have money?" Each fellow answered,

"No." The younger fellow said, "We might have a few coins on the floor of the car?" The older guy said, "I have a credit card that has maybe $3 left." I wished I could have helped financially, but when I run, I don't carry any form of money with me.

The owner stayed with his car, as I drove his partner to the gas station. A gallon of gas on that day sold for $2.69, so we filled the can close to full, costing $2.62. After the credit card transaction, there was $1.38 remaining, one dollar more than they thought. With the full gallon of gas added, the car started easily. The younger fellow said, "Thank you so much!" and both of them headed off with one gallon of gas and the meager amount on the credit card. Throughout our conversations, I found out that both were profoundly tired, having finished an overnight, physical job responsibility (which explained the limp) in the neighboring town of Butler and were passing through our town of Auburn and continuing west towards the town of Garrett. As they departed, I told them, "Travel safely," and I had confidence that God would continue to assist them.

After parking my car, I only had time to run about a half mile, return to the car, drive home, and get ready for our morning church service. Approximately one hour later I was driving my wife and me in the same car to our church. About two miles from our destination a sound went off from the car's dashboard. It was the "low on fuel" warning! *Yikes!* I had just recently been at the gas station, but I didn't have any money with me either! What a story that could have been, if I would have run out of gas helping the two gentlemen who were also out of gas!

Reflecting back on the entire episode, I felt God's presence throughout. My scheduled running plan got aborted for a while, but was resumed to a lesser degree later on. But the fellows' situation was more dire, with few options, if any. The younger guy was like a "stranger in a strange land, at a strange time of day." He was exhausted, limping along, with no money or functional car and decided to put faith in a much older guy, dressed in running clothing from head to toe, who was wearing a hydration belt loaded with bottles of water, and at least a half mile from home.

I was happy that through God's guidance I was able to help with their needs. In retrospect, I wished I would have helped a little more in some way. Two guys headed off down the road with minimum resources between them. When I recalled the entire story to Cathy, she said, "If I would have known, I would have invited them to our house and made them some breakfast." No doubt, she would have done that. After all, both of us were blessed with a set of parents who spent a good portion of their lives, role-modeling what giving to and helping others are all about. *Thank You, God, for our kind and generous parents, now deceased, Jack and Sharon for her and Harry and Lois for me!* Coincidently, all four stuck totally to their wedding vows of, "Until death do us part." Those strong bonds of dedication continued on both sides, even after the death of a spouse, as neither widowed partner remarried.

> *"When God's people are in need, be ready to help them.*
> *Always be eager to practice hospitality."*
> ROMANS 12:13

God's Peach – July 4, 2019

After that first Peachtree Road Race in 2006, which had both negative and positive consequences for me, I've been blessed to be able to run five more of these annual races on Independence Day in Atlanta, Georgia. To me, this event is so special because God's imprint is all over it! Being the world's largest 10K race, this year it attracted over 60,000 participants, an estimated 200,000 spectators, and 3,600 volunteers, who all blended together with an enormous amount of positive energy and enthusiasm. Being the fiftieth anniversary of this famous race added immensely to the race's spectacle.

Believing that we are all "children" of God, I had the opportunity to interact with thousands of God's kids all within a few hours in many unique ways. Riding shoulder-to-shoulder with fellow participants on the subway and in the shuttle bus at 6:30 in the morning started the day. Next, I mingled among thousands, as they walked from their public or private transportation to the race's epicenter in downtown Atlanta. Along the way, each participant had his own pre-race preparation, which included such necessities as walking, jogging, running, stretching, hydrating, or snacking.

Patriotism in the form of the National Anthem, an approximate 75-foot-long American flag hovering overhead affixed to a crane, and an Air Force flyover greeted all participants at the start line. Also included was a meaningful prayer asking for God's blessings of good health and safety for everyone. Immediately, from the beginning of the race I could see the effects of the spectators and volunteers, especially the security personnel, who made sure no traffic intersected our roadway. The spectators were so encouraging with their signs, noisemakers, and cheering. Even a priest in front of a church was sprinkling Holy Water for those who wished some.

At one point during my run, one of my shoelaces had come untied, even though it was double-knotted when the race began. It seemed like ten or twelve fellow runners thoughtfully and politely called my attention to the shoe issue, as they passed by me. God's messengers were helping me in the state of Georgia too! At the finish line and beyond was a horde of volunteers passing out the souvenir finisher's tee shirt, as well as icy towels and several necessary hydration and nutrition products. All of them added their own personal glow of inner spirit, while they congratulated tens of thousands of conquerors of this year's six miles of heat, humidity, and hills of Atlanta on this summer holiday. *Thank You, God, for that wonderful and most meaningful experience of being among so many of Your people, with Your presence, while celebrating life together!*

Wishing to give additional congratulations to this international event, I applauded native Kenyan, Rhonex Kipruto, for his Peachtree record time of 27 minutes and one second. This was also the best time ever achieved for that distance on American soil. He averaged only four minutes and 21 seconds per mile for over six miles! Of note, his brother finished in second place and fellow countrymen placed third, fifth, and tenth. It was, for sure, impressive and inspirational, especially since my time was about 40 minutes slower than his.

Other record-setting times were Brigid Kosgei, another Kenyan, in the women's division at 30:21, Brian Romanchuk in the men's wheelchair group at 18:11, and Manuela Schar in the women's wheelchair competition at 21:28. That was even more inspiration for me, as those hand-powered wheels negotiated the hills safely.

So, who benefitted the most from this major event? Was it the 60,752 people who took on the challenge, or the 60,637 finishers who received the special edition tee shirt? Was it the four category winners who received their normal prize money, in addition to the $50,000 bonus each got for setting a record? Was it the massive throng of spectators, like my wife Cathy and niece Cara, who positioned themselves about a half mile from the finish line with their cowbells and signs and cheered on thousands of participants? How about all the volunteers and race organizers who were so friendly and genuinely hospitable throughout the morning? My easy answer is that all of the above benefitted significantly, but my simplest answer is, "God smiled the most." He got to witness so many people, coming from all across the United States and from a wide variety of foreign lands, harmonizing together in common causes of fitness, peace, and goodwill.

> *"Be an example to all believers in what you say,*
> *in the way you live, in your love,*
> *your faith, and your purity."*
>
> 1 TIMOTHY 4:12

July 21

This Sunday started with some inspirational stories at our church. There were nine people, ranging in ages from kids to older adults, who each shared his or her story of finding faith and the love of God. Following each person's testimony was the water immersion baptism by one of our pastors or an inspirational leader, such as a youth director. Seeing some of the results of God's influence on these individuals was bonus motivation for me later in the day, when it was time for my run with God.

Three runners gave me additional motivation today on Auburn Drive. The first was a much younger and shorter guy than

I, perhaps in the 25 to 30 age range. I put him in the "racer" category, due to his much faster pace and the ease at which he was striding. Whereas I was doing my personal, straight-line journey of 1.8 miles each way, he did the same but then left the area for more running elsewhere. During the run, our paths crossed twice. While running west, I gave him a thumbs-up. After about another one and a half miles of running, while going east I acknowledged his accomplishment the same way. This time, he responded with a smile and a friendly head nod of appreciation.

A short time later came a young lady, also about the same age as the guy, and by my definition another "racer." Likewise, when our paths crossed, I gave her my thumbs-up encouragement. She responded verbally with, "You're doing well," a comment I appreciated deeply, especially on that humid day. My quick response was "You too!"

Near the end of my run for the day I saw in the distance a taller gentleman with a slimmer build, similar to mine. Like my usual pace, he was a "runner." I had seen him a few times at the YMCA, but I had not met him. It appeared that he set down his water bottle on the sidewalk for his return trip, rather than carry it. That gave me an indication that he would be coming back to that spot. Even though I was ready to "cool-down," jog, and then leave Auburn Drive for the day, I continued on a little farther.

Since I had been blessed and inspired by today's messengers from God, I thought perhaps, I could "play it forward" and be a messenger myself for this third person. I wasn't at my normal pace, but at least I could be a visual presence for him. I jogged an extra three-tenths of a mile so our paths would cross. I gave him a little wave, and he reciprocated with the same. From my perspective, it was God's mission accomplished.

As time has gone on, we have introduced ourselves, seen each other both at the Y and in the same neighborhood, and shared a number of common interest stories. My new friend Bob uses running to complement his other healthy lifestyle activities, some of which he teaches to other senior citizens. *Thank You, God, for those three people who motivated me on that day and for Bob's efforts to help others on a regular basis.*

July 30

On a Tuesday morning run, I chose to navigate the path that encircles the soccer fields north of the YMCA. There were only two walkers today, whom I had seen in the past. It appears they have a routine of getting some fresh air and exercise during a break time from work. They walk a short distance from their workplace. When each is by himself, there is eye contact with me on every lap. When together, they engage in active conversation throughout their walking laps. After saying, "Good morning," on the first pass and giving them my thumbs-up on the second and third laps, they smiled and gave me a thumbs-up, too! I admire their fitness commitment to their routine on a workday.

August 2

On Friday morning there were six individuals on that same course with me. I was happy to share this .8-mile path with a coach and three members of his cross-country team. Even though I did not know any of the teenage boys, I enjoyed watching their training nuances for improvement. On some laps, the coach followed the runners while riding his bicycle. On others, he kept close times on a stopwatch. This location worked efficiently for him, as he monitored their times on the west side of the large path and rode his bike across the common and parking lot area to the east side, where he got a second grouping of times. By cutting across the complex, he was able to get to each timing spot before his runners ran the periphery and crossed in front of him.

I felt blessed to have the opportunity to run on the same course with these athletes. They were so respectful of sharing space with me, even though they were on a focused mission for improvement. My thumbs-up encouragement on nearly every lap was greeted by smiles and nods from them. On one lap, I gave them all high fives as we passed. At one point, the coach said to me, "You're doing well!" Since I wasn't expecting his comment, my quick response was a simple "Thanks" as I ran by. It was a remarkably meaningful time spent with those youngsters and their coach.

Other messengers from God on that day were a guy who was walking and a lady who was bike-riding. The results were much the same for the walker. A thumbs-up from me elicited a smile from him. As the biker went zooming past, she certainly wasn't expecting any acknowledgment from me. After a smile and a wave from me on the first passing and a thumbs-up on the second and third ones, she smiled as she went by on that third pass.

Overall, it was a pleasant run with a mixture of positive motivators to spiritually help me along my way. *Thank You, God, for those people today. Each inspired me in a different and helpful way.*

"So encourage each other and build each other up . . ."

1 THESSALONIANS 5:11

August 6

On the first Tuesday morning in August, the humidity was high and there was a high probability for much-needed rain. I saw one speed runner coming from Auburn Drive into the Mason's Village subdivision running on the sidewalk in front of several houses. Even though our paths did not cross, he was an inspiration for me with his level of focus and pace, as he ran around the cul-de-sac.

Along came a second runner, whom I had seen before. With his easy stride and faster pace than mine, he was definitely in the "racer" mode too. Soon after my entry onto Auburn Drive, he was running west, as I headed east towards County Road 35. Whenever I see him, he gets a thumbs-up. I truly appreciated his acknowledgment when he said, "Nice job!" This inspiration took on a heartfelt meaning for me, especially with our apparent age differential being in the range of 30 to 35 years.

Continuing east I noticed immediately the high humidity and heavy air. My initial thoughts were that I needed to monitor my body and its water intake a little closer than usual and to be open to the possibility that my distance goal that day might not be reached.

I finished my eastern run to County Road 35, touched the symbolic stop sign, turned around and headed west. My first thought was, *Thank You, God!* There was a light, cooling breeze coming from the west. Once again, God gave me what

I needed, when I needed it. Even though the breeze gave me some additional wind resistance, it was a bit refreshing.

August 21 – Lady in Green

Today's Wednesday goal was an intended run for distance, rather than speed, to continue to build up my base in anticipation of my ten-plus-mile adventure in late September. Hoping my body parts would agree, my goal was to run at least six miles, if time allowed. My course today was the pathway north of the YMCA facility and around the soccer fields.

There was only one of God's messengers during my time there. It was a young lady dressed primarily in green. Walking was her choice of exercise, and we went in opposite directions around the course. On our first eye-to-eye passing, we shared a "Good morning." On our second and third "meetings" I gave her my standard thumbs-up. She nodded following the former and gave me a thumbs-up after the latter. On the fourth encounter I gave her again the same sign and told her, "Good job!" She responded with another matching sign and smiled. With her mission apparently complete, she left the course and headed for the YMCA building. *God, I appreciated the one messenger You put on my path today as inspiration. I hoped with Your urgings, I was able to do something beneficial for her.*

August 23 – Dedicated Caregiver

Today was a light workout for the legs, primarily walking a couple laps around the YMCA building, for a total of about one and a half miles. In that short time, I was inspired at a high level. I saw a young lady pushing a stroller with a single child resting comfortably in it. This lady definitely had a game plan. When I first saw her, she was running while pushing the stroller. This was followed by a short distance of walking while pushing. Then she ran and pushed, before cooling off with another walk. She continued diligently with some form of running-pushing or walking-pushing without stopping. I admired her dedication and multi-tasking efforts!

On our passing during my first lap, I gave her a thumbs-up and a smile. She was going too fast to respond. On my second lap, I gave her the same sign and told her, "You're doing great!" She acknowledged with a smile. Later I thought, Wow, *what dedication! Perhaps, I should have continued on the path to give her some additional positive reinforcement?* But my mission that day was to do some activities inside the building. *Thank You, God, for today's inspiration. That was impressive, indeed!*

August 28

My Wednesday goals were minimal today, as this was my last training run before my next race, only three days away. An easy beginning, some pace in the middle, and a relaxed finish highlighted the workout. The first lap (.8 mile) included walking, jogging, and running. That lap was followed by two laps of running at desired race day pace, which included my motto, "Trust God, just do it." The last lap consisted of jogging and walking to finish up the session.

To finish out a race week, I typically walk about a mile two days before a race, solely to keep my movement metabolism going. On the day before a race, I try to lead a slow-paced life-style with no walking or running laps at all.

Today, while I was out on the course, I received some "book thoughts," some of which I've shared on this page. Lately, this seems to be a regular occurrence . . . Run with God and go home and let God "move" my pen. *Thank You, God, for Your partnership today!*

August 31 – Parade and Race Day

Each year our small town of Auburn (population near 13,000) has over 10,000 visitors daily during the Labor Day weekend. Our town used to design and manufacture Auburn and Cord automobiles in the early 1900s and design the classic Duesenberg muscle cars. We celebrate that heritage with the annual Auburn-Cord-Duesenberg Festival. A long list and wide variety of events dominate the week-long event that culminates on Labor Day Monday.

In addition to the four days of car auctioneering, there is also a "Parade of Classics," where up to 300 vintage automobiles will "strut" their colors, chrome, size, and early 1900s designs through downtown Auburn, slowly, of course, on a Saturday. As thousands of spectators arrive early to "stake out" their favorite and unobstructed viewing spots along the parade route, many are positioned to watch runners and walkers who participate in the 5K (3.1 mile) race or the 2K (1.2 mile) family walk.

This pre-parade event is surrounded by the classic car culture of our town. Cars and spectators are everywhere. The racecourse goes through the hub of the city and around the beautifully-adorned courthouse square, which includes a historic heritage courthouse with numerous marble influences on the inside. The races that run through the "heart" of this town, as well as the races in July in downtown Atlanta and the one in late September through Fort Wayne are uplifting to me. Not only do I get the historical flavor of each of these famous locales, but I also experience the cultural essence and "heartbeat" of the citizens who organize and support major events to exude the pride they have for living where they do.

"Now you have light from the Lord.
So live as people of light! For this light within you
produces only what is good and right and true."
EPHESIANS 5:8-9

As a runner of this Labor Day weekend race, I always feel blessed by God to be able to participate, honored to be a part of the holiday events as a performer, and energized by so many spectators who support the walkers and runners. Additionally, I like the prayer at the beginning of this Auburn race, which helps me focus on my run with God. Also addressed is the hope of God's "protective shield" to allow all participants the opportunity to have a safe and healthy race. For the past eleven years this Saturday morning event has been sponsored by a local Christian-based ministry called Lakewood Park Christian School. When I write a check for entry into this race, I always feel totally confident that LPCS and God, working together, will utilize those funds for the benefit of God's children in some way.

The organizers were pleased that there were over 100 participants motivated to improve their fitness and help a worthy cause. By design, I started the race typically a little slower than my desired pace for the majority of the run. Historically, this allows me time to "settle in" to a comfort zone for my body mechanics, without being influenced by the speeds of the much faster runners.

There have been races in the past where excitement and adrenaline "kicked in" at the race's onset and I started too fast for my abilities. The results gave me some impressive times during the first mile or two, but with major fatigue and struggle moments later, as I simply tried to get to the finish line! Gaining perhaps a minute or so at the beginning is not worth needing an extra four or five minutes at the end.

With my gradual build-up of speed, I reached my desired race pace and kept it throughout most of the three miles. At approximately the 2.5-mile mark, with only a little more than a half mile to go, I began to assess all my body parts and related variables, internally and externally, to consider a finisher's kick. When I decided that all systems were ready to go, I began to tweak up the speed a little, moving my feet a little faster without changing my stride or posture. In the past, sometimes an increased stride has caused added stress to my hamstrings, for example.

Of course, I made sure God was "on board" for not only this racing upgrade, but also during the final fifth of a mile, when I made my strongest remaining efforts. "Trust God, just do it" was again my battle cry, as I put Him in charge to take us both to the finish line, which He did. With the age of my body parts, I definitely put myself in a risk-taking mode, but there was a great deal of comfort for me finishing the race with Him, as always.

Since our pastor's message on the topic of "Trust God, just do it" about three years ago, I have been able to have a "strong" finish at the end of nearly every race with God's presence felt on every step. Frequently, I have found that because of my finishes, the second half of my races are run at faster times than the first half, which is somewhat unusual for the majority of distance runners, whose results I've seen or with whom I've spoken.

It was unbelievably surprising to me that this was also evident in my most physically demanding race of the year, the Peachtree Road Race. In downtown Atlanta on July Fourth, typically the heat and humidity indices are both close to 80, and the major and most significant hills are in the second half of the race. Sometimes, my split times for the 10K race show a respectable difference of between 30 seconds to a full minute faster on the back half of the race. Some might say, "Huh?" or "Go figure that one out!" For me, it's simply, *make sure I take God with me to the end.*

> "The Lord is like a father to his children,
> tender and compassionate . . ."
> PSALM 103:13

September 10

Today I finished my run and goals on the course around the Sports Complex north of the YMCA building. In my walking-cool down mode, I finished the short, north-south pathway that "connects" the two venues. Walking westward toward the Y's entry driveway where I would cross North Street, I noticed a lady walking eastwardly on the other side of the street. Rarely, do I make any acknowledgment of an exerciser that far away, especially with the usual great deal of vehicle traffic, including delivery semi-trucks, that separates the two parallel sidewalk areas.

However, on that day, I felt an urging to be aware of the lady. I had seen her twice in the past week doing her walking routine on the pathway around the Y building. I gave her my standard thumbs-up bit of encouragement, and she smiled back. I sensed she needed to make some eye contact to assist her in some way. So I did and smiled back at her. She continued east, and I finished my walk going west, crossed the street, entered the parking lot, and then drove home. I trusted God totally that what little I did was necessary for her at that moment.

September 23 – Race Day Prep

One of my favorite race days, which is sponsored by the organization called Fort4Fitness, comes on the last Saturday of September in Fort Wayne, Indiana. With expansion over the past 12 years, they now offer four different races on that morning, ranging in distance from four miles to a full marathon of over 26 miles. The start times of these races are spaced well enough so that a person could run multiple races, if so desired. This year (2019), I planned to run the two shortest races and was training appropriately for them.

Late September in northeastern Indiana can bring a wide range of conditions and temperatures for this race day, especially for an early morning start time. Some years, the temperature has been in the mid-40-degree Fahrenheit range, but this year it appeared that our northeast Indiana version of "Indian Summer" was going to hit during the week of the race. My first training run that week actually landed on the official day of fall's arrival, Monday, September 23. I was pleased with the temperature of 63 degrees, with the humidity at ninety-two percent due to an early morning rain. While some would prefer lower numbers in one or both categories, I thanked God for giving me those conditions. I felt my body could use a sweat-cleansing and secondly, this could help acclimate me to elements I might encounter a few days later.

As I was running east on Auburn Drive, I saw my first motivator, an older man, whom I had seen many times around town and at the YMCA, but never on this road. He was walking westward when our steps landed on the same piece of sidewalk. I said, "Good morning!" His response was like none other I had ever heard. He said, "There is no finish line. You know that!" *Whoa, where did that come from and what exactly did it mean?* I don't recall, if he had that finger-pointing aspect of a parent giving a son or daughter a stern lesson, but the tone of his voice was definitely parental and advising.

As I continued at my same pace, I analyzed his comments more and more. My only conclusion was that he was judging my speed and age with the existing conditions. I gave him the benefit of the doubt that he was trying to be a helpful older adult, recommending me to slow down. Hmm . . . Interesting scenario, as I continue my daily journey towards my seventieth birthday! *(Even though both my parents have passed on, perhaps I have another parental figure out there looking after me? Perhaps sent by God?)*

Since we had never met in a running or walking scenario or anywhere, actually, I don't think he noticed that I was wearing a hydration belt loaded with water bottles and nutrition to meet my needs for a longer, faster run. And the pace I ran was the target pace I planned to run for my ten miles a few days later. Ironically, his mention of "no finish line" was, for sure, the opposite of my goals for race day, as I hoped to actually cross the end line for each of the two races.

After I reached my eastward destination at County Road 35, touched the stop sign, and turned around to go west, I noticed he was still walking in the same westward direction. I thought, God, *I need to say something to him, when I pass by, that is positive with a soft, light tone of voice, while maintaining my running pace.* Stopping to have a discussion was probably not appropriate. As I passed him, I looked at him and said, "Have a nice day!" His response was "Yes!" which I clearly detected had a more upbeat tone than before.

God, thank You for the intersection of that guy with me today and for the learning opportunity for both of us. I sensed that each of us had a few minutes to reflect on that first "meeting." He seemed to soften his viewpoint and perhaps saw that I was, with God's help, prepared for the circumstances. For me, I was able to maintain calmness and patience as a personal growth experience and, moving forward, I held no grudge against him.

September 28 – Race Day

On race day Saturday, I awoke at 5 a.m., left the house at 6, drove to Fort Wayne, and parked the car at 6:40. Rain had ended but was still hovering in the area, as the humidity was in the ninety-two to ninety-three percent range. The temperature at race time was between 67 and 69 degrees. At 7:20 my hat was off for the National Anthem, and I heard a meaningful prayer for safety and nice weather for the approximate 10,000 participants for the four morning races. A cannon start began both of my races at 7:30 and 10:30.

With the two races (6.2 miles and 4 miles) and warm-ups and cool-downs for each, and walking around the baseball stadium, where all races finished at the home plate area, it was easily a 12-mile morning for my legs, lungs, heart, and lesser affected body parts. Prior to this race day, none of my training sessions this year was more than seven or eight miles, and there were only a few of those. My mindset was that I was doing a six-mile race, to be followed by proper reloading of nutrition and hydration, and then stretching and warm-up movement, before running a four-mile race. This game plan has suited my aging body better than doing one race at ten or more miles.

Of the three major components—mind, body, and spirit—I consider the spiritual element to be the most important. A strong body without inspiration, motivation, and passion will not find its highest level of performance. As I described in my previous book, if I am standing next to a more athletic person and there's a ball on the floor 30 feet away, I expect the athlete to get to the ball quicker than I do. My only chance to "win" that challenge is if he is not motivated to perform at his best. If my spiritual component is peaked and his is not, then I have at least a chance to out-perform the better gifted and trained athlete.

Having God "on board" for my races definitely enhanced my spiritual abilities. For each of those races, I crossed the start line saying, *With You, God.* The races were run around several Fort Wayne neighborhoods before entering the professional minor league baseball park. After entering the stadium in the left field corner and running the warning track around the outfield, I concluded each race with the "homestretch" run from the right field foul line to the finish line, which sat directly above the well-covered home plate. For both races I was able to get into my mindset of, "Trust God, just do it," about a half mile before the end line. I was blessed, as I neared the end of each race, to be able to increase my pace a little after the last turn for home, and I thanked God for going the distance with me.

Whenever I increase my pace, there is always a risk factor.

My breathing, and any of the hundred or so body parts I use, are affected, which can be an issue for a guy my age. Since I started the race with God, there was no reason to "abort" the mission. I had Him with me to the end of both races. Any risk factors or burdens, I felt, went from my shoulders to His. My faith and trust in Him overrode any physical limitations. Actually, my motto about trusting God became rhythmic, as did my accelerated breathing.

This rhythmic concept is similar to the final stretch run of the famous horse, Secretariat, as he was winning his third race to complete horse racing's Triple Crown in 1973. His stride and breathing, as depicted in the Hollywood movie by the same horse's name, were seemingly in perfect balance, and the horse's "kick" at the end of the race continued to add more and more distance between him and the rest of the competing horses, which led to a record-setting winning margin.

Although I don't win any races and I am certainly not at the athletic level of that special horse, when my motto about God is in tune with my breathing and pace, the finishes of my races are generally quite strong, at least from Cathy's vantage point. She is usually at or near the end of my six-mile races, which is reinforcement for her and incentive for me that I survived the race's variables.

Because I'm still in a race mode "kick" when I cross a finish line, my facial appearance doesn't show my ecstatic exuberance on the inside, that God and I together have finished the race we started. Having seen some examples of the professional photographers' finish line photos of me, I have noticed that "needing medical attention" look now and then. Fortunately, spending time with the med staff after a race has only happened once, and that is truly enough!

I still like to run competitively, not to win any prizes but simply to compete against myself. Running gives me that challenge with so many variables and circumstances that offer me the opportunity to "master" my moments. No two moments, days, races, or conditions are ever the same. When I ran the race in early July in Atlanta, I accomplished the city's downtown 6.2-mile course in over 67 minutes. Then, in late September in Fort Wayne, my race time for the same distance was just over 62 minutes.

There were many differences between the two races, but for both I was pleased. God was with me spiritually, and, combined with my mental mindset, I was able to "push" my body through the many challenges of those two special races. I finished each in a healthy and injury-free manner. Another monitor for me is the overall effect the race had on my body, which shows up during my post-race recovery. Sore muscles that appear within the first 48 hours after a race are a good sign for me. That is an indication that the spiritual and mental components got the physical aspect to perform close to its peak ability. If I finish a race in a healthy manner, and I get no soreness after it, then I consider if I could have put a little more effort into that event.

Frequently, after a race, friends and runners will ask, "How did the race go?" I usually tell them how the experience went, and then I add, "Check back with me in a couple days," so we can assess the overall effects of the race on me physically.

God's Helpers

When I run a race, oh my, there is so much to be thankful for! Not only all the logistical aspects, but also the setting, uniqueness, and special conditions of that particular event. Not to mention, of course, all the people involved, which includes the sponsors and organizers, as well as the many volunteers! I thank God for all of these individuals, whose contributions make a particular race possible. During a race, even if I am "huffing and puffing" during some of my miles, I try to thank as many volunteers along the way as I can. To me, they are God's messengers sent on that particular day, to use the talents that He has given them, to help other human beings in His world.

The most obvious helpers are those who assist at the hydration and nutrition stations. But also important to the cause are those who provide first aid and safety along any racing venue. At my larger events, there are countless local law enforcement officials and military personnel stationed at nearly every intersection, covering several miles. I consider their placement along a race route to be a godsend strategy to accentuate their talents, display His gift of love, and exemplify the beautiful touch of the Holy Spirit within them. Their mission is clear to me: to help as many people as possible while working for God and doing those tasks He needs done at that moment. Even more, they perform those good deeds without complaint or fanfare. Another area for an abundance of helpers is at the finish line and beyond, where so many assist tired participants. The passion of God's helpers to serve is perhaps at a higher level than mine is to run and thank them.

Therefore, my race day mission is always twofold: to partner with God to run the best race possible with the given variables and to verbally thank as many volunteers as I can during the race, as well as those serving at the pre- and post-race times. I am especially grateful for those who make the extra effort to complement a race on a holiday. At my largest race in Atlanta, there are over 3,600 volunteers to help make that event one of the world's most unique. Of the two- hundred thousand supportive spectators and musicians, who line the six-plus miles of streets, I try to recognize as many as possible with a simple wave, head nod, smile, or by saying, "Thank you."

I get positive, uplifting feelings from all the participants I am exposed to throughout the long morning adventure. In addition to travelling with many on the metro subway system prior to the race, I share a vast amount of common ground during the entire race day experience. Last year's race included over 60, 000 participants, including wheelchair racers and elite international runners, in addition to the wide variety of runners and walkers. I see all of them and me as God's children. I enjoy sharing my time and space with them, boarding the subway system, then running the race, and later on cheering encouragement for others. What a wonderful and full morning of interaction with so many from different states and countries! *Thank You, God, for all who make this day such a memorable success for so many, and I am so blessed for all those who intersect my paths today.*

Every human being I see on my running journey is meaningful to me and a special "messenger" sent by God. Whether our paths cross early or late, or somewhere in the middle, each person is a boost or a "pick me up" of inspiration and motivation. I see God's spiritual handiwork in each of them, which motivates me to keep going, one step after the other.

> *"And what a relief to see your friendly smile.*
> *It is like seeing the face of God!"*
> GENESIS 33:10

RESPECTING GOD'S CREATURES

8

Sidewalk Friends

Even though August in northeastern Indiana can sometimes be a little hot and sultry, there are usually some days that give a hint of the oncoming fall season. On the fourth day of this month, I noticed my first grasshoppers jumping out from the fields and onto the adjacent sidewalk where I was running. *Welcome back little creatures, and welcome to fall!*

While running on August 6, I saw my first "woolly" worms (caterpillars) leave land and venture onto the sidewalks. Butterflies became more abundant in the areas where I ran. Ant and spider varieties are more common, and I see them on a regular basis, except in the winter months.

Regardless of which type of living organisms enter the path I'm on, my philosophy is to embrace them as purposeful creatures in God's kingdom and to do my best to not interfere with their lives. This gets to be a challenge at times, when one unexpectedly comes in front of me, either in the air or on the pavement. Sometimes when that happens, I have little or no time to react to avoid striking them with a body part or with the next running step. Even though I probably shouldn't have, I have broken stride and nearly tripped a few times to keep from stepping on a little creature.

The greatest challenge is after a recent rain, when many earthworms are driven from the soggy soil and are inching their way across the sidewalk. Also quite challenging is when grasshoppers "spring" from land to sidewalk, or from one sidewalk square to another with their totally erratic flying and landing patterns. Sometimes their leaping height is up to my waist, and other times they land right where my next foot is prepared to step!

Woodland Friends

God's larger creatures require a different focus to maintain health and safety for all. On one early morning run I saw a family of deer, consisting of two large and three small ones. They came out of the east end of the woods, about 80 yards from Auburn Drive, and headed south where they could cross the road and enter the woods on the other side. The family moved slowly and cautiously on a narrow strip of land between the woods and an open field.

My vantage point was about 100 yards to the east as I was running west from the County Road 35 intersection. If the deer and I continued on our same paces, our paths could have likely crossed on the sidewalk where I was running. I decided to avoid that possibility, since one never knows what an animal (or human) might do when startled.

My game plan was to slow down or even stop well ahead of a potential sidewalk collision, to allow the family to continue to their apparent goal. However, I sensed immediately that the family had stopped and would not move again until the "coast was clear." It appeared the deer family was not taking any chances and wanted to dictate how this situation might play out.

With no movement from any of them and all five "frozen" in place like statues, I decided to not only get to the intersection point first, but also to accelerate my pace to clear the "zone" and allow God's beautiful running creatures their freedom to roam to the other side of Auburn Drive. I felt God's presence highlighting my day with the appearance of this woodland family and in urging us to honor each other respectfully.

I have not seen any other live four-legged creatures during my runs there. Some exist, of course, as I have seen the results of their demise on that road surface. Nocturnal animals such as racoons, groundhogs, and opossums have evidently tried unsuccessfully to cross the east-west road going from one part of the woods to the other.

When I notice roadkill remains, I thank God for each animal's existence, hoping that each had a purposeful life in God's scheme of earthly matters. I pray at that moment that each, in its now-altered physical state, can serve other creatures of God as some type of nourishment to help them in survival mode. I have seen much evidence of this, especially benefitting the flying species of insects and birds, both large and small. Since I do not run after dark, I can only assume that nocturnal animals also benefit from a former woodland animal's demise.

Frequent Flyers

I have noticed on a somewhat regular basis, especially during early Sunday morning runs, usually two or three remarkably large and loud crows perched on a treetop overlooking Auburn Drive. They always seem to notice me, as I hear their bellowing caws of communication. At times they sound menacing, as if discussing me as their preference for breakfast! Even though sometimes they travel east or west with me, gliding from treetop to treetop, they have not swooped down in my direction, yet! Due to their size and sound, they definitely have my full attention, and I glance at them often, to make sure they don't surprise me from behind! Even though they have that potential, I assume the best and that they are sent from God. *Thank You for being with me this morning and giving me protection, as I run this stretch of roadway.*

New Courses

Recent additions to my running locales include a .7-mile path around our county YMCA facility, as well as an .8-mile path around a sports complex across the street from the Y. This complex of James Park was built by the Y, which also sponsors seven soccer fields and maintains a spacious pond and parking lot. I enjoy each course for different reasons. The shorter course is rectangular in shape, with rounded corners. With the Y building in the center, there can be some helpful wind blockage at times. Across the street, the longer path is shaped more like two letter "L's" whose long sides are back-to-back. This configuration includes eight turns for each completed lap. What I like most about this course is that I am constantly changing directions and adjusting to the wind element each time, especially in this wide-open panorama.

Since the larger venue has a rather expansive pond inside the perimeter path, it attracts waterfowl, primarily geese and ducks. During migration times, some fly in to use the facilities for brief stays and then fly out. Others "hang-out" for a much longer period of time using the YMCA as their home base. During the summer months, for example, I saw these "homesteaders" nearly every time I ran on either of the Y's two paths. Since the sports complex is only .2 mile from the YMCA building, the geese have free reign to inhabit wherever they choose and still be close to the pond. On many occasions during my runs, some of the geese are crossing one of the paths where I am running, or they have recently, as evidenced by their droppings. Either way, I see them as God's creatures planted there purposely to help me practice patience and improve my running agility and focus. They are beautiful to watch, especially when in flight with full wingspans, and also when they coast in for a pond landing!

God's Beauty

Even though there are fewer wooded areas close to the YMCA than on Auburn Drive, I have adapted to and now immensely enjoy my recently discovered courses. The pond that is surrounded on three sides by the trail I use is scenic, especially with the waterfowl that use it. To the north is a narrow forest line, which helps separate properties while providing some privacy. Additionally, there are open fields to the west of the facility, and park benches adorn the trail route within the complex. While I have not seen any woodland creatures yet, I do appreciate a plethora of butterflies I see during my runs.

On one of my runs, one particular butterfly caught my attention. It was the orange monarch type. My trek on that day was to go counter-clockwise around the "double L-shaped" path. On my first lap going north, I noticed the flyer on the approximate .1-mile segment. But I thought nothing of it, since I had seen others of the same variety. When I returned to the same segment of pathway, I did not notice it right away, because it was resting on the asphalted path with its wings closed and blending into the sidewalk scenery.

As I approached, its wings opened laterally, and it flew a short distance to my left (west) and lit on the grass. *Hmm . . . interesting. Could it be the same one I saw when I came through here about ten minutes ago?* So, I continued and ran another lap. As I turned right to go up the northern section again, I actually started to look for my "flying friend." When I had run about three-quarters of that portion of pavement and didn't see him, I thought, *Ok, coincidences are over . . . case closed . . . time to refocus on my running!*

Then, like before, he was perched on the pathway, camouflaged, with wings closed. He then opened up and fluttered again to the grassy area to my left. *Wow,* I thought, *could this truly be another messenger moment from God?* From my perspective the answer was, *Yes!* On that day I came through that area four more times, and each time was a carbon-copy performance.

He was positioned on the trail at approximately the same spot every time and moved only when I got close, always venturing to the same grassy side. *Coincidence?* I don't think so . . .

seven times out of seven with the same behavior. *Did he have some reason to go to the same area?* None, that I could see. There were no flowers, bushes, trees, food sources, or aromas to be found on the smooth trail or the recently-mown grass! God's message to me was, *Keep doing what you are doing. I am on the trail with you!* What a comfort!

Butterfly Freedom

I have to admit that butterflies have taken on a new meaning and perspective for me in the past five years. God blessed me with two wonderful, role-modeling parents who were likewise blessed by living over 80 years each. This included 61 years of marriage to each other. Since they both passed due to natural causes, they had time to discuss their end-of-life intentions with us, their five sons. Each parent died four years apart, almost to the day, Mom on an Easter Sunday and Dad a couple days after Easter. They requested that their ash remains be mixed together to symbolize their long union and then dispersed from a mountain top in the northern region of the state of Georgia. Within six weeks of the second parent's passing, we sons were able to find an appropriate location and carried out their final wishes.

After some preliminary ceremonies, thoughts, and prayers at the site, we released the remains down a mountain side. Immediately from that same location, two butterflies came spiraling upwards and toward our overlook. What a moment for all of us to see! The spiraling reminded me of the interconnectedness of strands of DNA and the forever linking of our parents.

To me, it was a message from God saying, *All is well. They are safe with me!* Today, when I see the fluttering beauty of butter-flies, I think of the freedom my parents now have from their earthly ailments.

> *"Then God looked over all he had made,*
> *and he saw that it was very good!"*
>
> GENESIS 1:31

FINISHING WITH GOD

9

McIntyre Mile

Nearing the end of a run, with that day's goals generally met and with some level of fatigue, my motivation to finish strongly on a "high note" was to honor God and thank Him for His blessings on my running journey. I did this by singing a short paraphrase from a tune frequently sung at our church referring to the world and the cross. Even though I don't sing well, this tune and its meaning gave me a focus directed at God.

Since this ending episode of my run is so spiritually motivating, I frequently add some thoughts. As a base, I sing these words three times: "the world behind me, the cross before me," and then conclude with another phrase, "no turning back," which I sing twice. With modifications, I add some additional thoughts: *the world (with its challenges, conflicts, adversities, etc.) behind me . . . the cross (faith, hope, God's helping hands, etc.) before me.* This is my singing slogan when I turn left onto McIntyre Drive coming from Duesenberg Drive. This intersection is approximately one-third of a mile from my entry into our cul-de-sac. As I sing, I extend both hands forward at chest height, reaching out, as if to touch and hold "the cross before me."

This symbolic and spiritual final "push" gives me an added "spark" to put forth a little extra energy, as I approach my personal "finish line." These words and thoughts, along with the focus on God and the cross, always bring a smile to my face and an added sense of peace and comfort. God has always been with me when I start that day and at the end, too! Sometimes I run the length of the cul-de-sac and return to its intersection point with the street (an additional two-tenths mile). Occasionally, I run our "keyhole" cul-de-sac a second time. And if I feel like I have a little more "left in the tank," I run an extra length and use my motto, "Trust God, just do it," as fatigue reaches its peak.

Basically, I push myself one final time for that day's run and put God's will totally in charge. Saying that phrase and trusting God during my most fatiguing moments of the day are total spiritual bliss for me! Upon completion, my arms come up, as if I am a runner "breaking" the tape and winning a race. *Only in my dreams, of course!* My cool-down jog and eventual walking pace follow immediately to complete my day's training.

Even though I run with a great deal of awareness of my surroundings and like to spend that one-on-one time with God over several miles, I thoroughly enjoy that finishing mile or so. No matter how far I have run or what type of workout I have done, McIntyre Drive is a "home" base for me. Here, every step, fast or slow, had a special meaning, especially when centered around God.

Spiritual Grands

Another spiritual aspect that is important to me is the love and devotion that I have for our grandchildren. The blessings of being able to have children is a godsend. Unfortunately, not everybody is able to experience that. Then, for our children to also have children of their own adds another layer of blessings to all of our family members. Many years ago my dad said to me, "Just wait until you have grandkids. It will be the most enjoyable part of your life." And he was right. What a blessed life it has been since the first one arrived 12 years ago!

R and R

Seeing the letter "R" complement itself has brought a lot of concepts to me and, I'm sure, to others over the years. As a youngster I learned to find where a restroom or the nearest railroad crossing was. Then at school it was the colloquial "reading, 'riting, and 'rithmetic." Getting older, I learned the necessity of "rest and recuperation." Now, in my much older years, I like to pair "reading" and "running" together.

If there is one small bit of wisdom that I have tried to pass on to our child-rearing kids, it is the value of both reading and running. It appears, so far, that these R's have been emphasized as a base for our grandkids' development. Hopefully, each "R" can be enjoyed at some level rather than being a task-oriented burden. My first premise is that much of present-day education, and life in general, has some level of a reading component within it, especially in today's "information age," with a high level of social media.

I wish that when I grew up I had a higher level of fondness for reading. Since I didn't, subjects like history and literature, and even all those story problems in math, were a greater challenge for me. Even though math was probably my favorite subject area, leading to consistently high grades in school, those story problems were solvable, but still a "pain in the posterior." History and literature never had a chance to make my all-time list of favorite subjects! For both, I had to put in a lot of extra effort to earn a "B" or "C" letter grade. I can't remember ever getting an "A" in either of those subjects from seventh grade studies through college graduation.

From that time until the present, I have had a deeper passion and a more in-depth appreciation for both subjects, and I am now engaged with them on an almost daily basis. I am very proud that our five oldest grandkids (ages two through eleven) appear to like to read and seek out that activity often, even when surrounded by many other choices. Kudos to all parents everywhere who find a way to encourage the youngest generation about the long-term, positive effects of reading.

The other "R" is running. I certainly don't expect any of our six grandkids to be a fantastic distance runner or sprinter. That is not the goal. But if each can gain an appreciation to view running as a "fun" activity and not as "drudgery," then I think that improves each person's opportunity to maintain some positive level of mind-body-spirit balance.

Running promotes movement, which the body is designed to do naturally. Enjoying running or movement at a core level has enormous potential to lead one away from sedentary lifestyles, which seem to be growing trends in the fitness levels of our USA population. Like reading, attaining the habit of moving, especially in the early years, can pay healthy dividends throughout one's life.

Running and winning races is not nearly as important as enjoying any kind of movement skills and appreciating the many benefits that come over time. So far, our six grandchildren, who represent four different families, are all into movement at some level. Whether it is walking, hiking, running, or sprinting (in sports), they are finding some degree of enjoyment in their movements. The oldest four grandkids (Kelsea, James, Sawyer, and Andrew) appear to take some pride in running, especially as fast as possible. One-year-old Antonio has recently begun to walk. Two-year-old Emma, named after Emma Gatewood, the first female to hike the entire Appalachian Trail, has not caught the "running bug" yet, but loves to hike hills and mountains. With her parents and brother, she has progressed to two-mile hikes so far. Even three-year old Andrew, who has a larger body frame with shorter legs and doesn't seem to have the typical runner's leaner look, takes on his self-given nickname, "cheetah," when he runs! *God bless his enthusiasm!*

> "When you affirm big, believe big,
> and pray big, big things happen."
> NORMAN VINCENT PEALE, American Minister and Author

At some point in the future I will start "planting" some seeds with those grandkids about the importance and value of taking God with them on their journeys. I am hopeful that each will feel His presence during their movement activity and experience the comfort and encouragement He can give them, especially when their focus is in His direction. In recent years as our grandchild population has expanded quickly with five births within the past five years, I have added them spiritually to my runs, especially in competition. Those kids can give me an extra "boost" when needed during a race. My most challenging races now are the 10K events, which feature six-plus miles.

6 - 4 - 6

Since we have those six grandkids, I "take them along" on my races. So, with God "on board," I dedicate one mile to each of them. Mile one thoughts with personal motivation go to our youngest (Antonio), and the extremely important final mile dedication goes to our oldest (Kelsea). She understands the beauty and benefits of running herself. When I need a little extra "boost" to get to my finish line, I am reminded of watching her efforts to get to her finish line at the end of her annual triathlon (swimming, biking, running). She also exudes energy and encouragement as she completes competition in her team sports, such as basketball, softball, and volleyball. Her excellent focus and dedication to the end of an activity or school project is also an inspiration for me.

For the other four grandkids (Emma, Andrew, Sawyer, and James, ages two, three, four, and five, respectively), I think of their stories so far with movement skills and what influence I might be able to add to their lives going forward. Then, when the timing is right, I plan to relate my experiences of "running with God" to them. Hopefully, we'll see where that concept leads them, as it blends in with the influences of their parents, schools, and their church-related and other community resources.

During my dedicated mile for each of them, I pray that all their movement skills continue to develop and that each can someday bond with God in a positive way that is pleasing to both sides. With God's help, the six-grandkids-for-six-miles concept works well for me right now and reminds me that His blessings have provided me with both those youngsters and those miles in my life.

"Now all glory to God, who is able,
through his mighty power at work within us, to accomplish
infinitely more than we might ask or think."
EPHESIANS 3:20

When I run a shorter race, such as a three or a four-miler, I still focus on all the grandkids, and I simply refer to two of them per mile. Again, it is not important that each takes up the physical act of running, but rather that they explore until they find what works well for them. Whether they walk, hike, bike, swim, hop, skip, climb, or run, my hope is that they discover God's presence and "run" with His guiding hand, as they pursue their activities throughout their lives.

Balancing Life

While not easily attained, I believe that the goal of mind-body-spirit balanced living is to be equally strong in all three major areas. Understandably, there are other factors involved in a well-balanced life, such as the emotional and psychological elements, to name a couple. I consider these and other aspects to be tangential to the core triangle of mind-body-spirit. I like to compare this equilateral triangle with the color triangle, with everything starting with the primary three of red, blue, and yellow. Then, when triangle parts are blended together, life and beauty have purpose and function.

As stated in my previous book, striving for a calm, clear mind, a relaxed body, and a passionate, motivated spirit can lead to an improvement in one's quality of life. Of course, God's presence can profoundly influence all three areas, especially at a high level in the spirit category. I have found that the effect of the Holy Spirit has contributed significantly to increased levels of desire and motivation to keep my mind and body strong and sound to do what God wants me to do. I have sensed for a long time that the healthier I am in these three main areas, the more opportunities He gives me to serve others, in addition to the degree to which I can benefit God's people in some way.

Power of the Mind

At a martial arts training workshop once, our grandmaster said that if you don't control your own mind, someone or something else will. After the session, I inquired further with him about the workings of the mind, asking him if it ever stops. His response was that the mind never rests, even when we sleep. This information complemented substantially what my martial arts master said about 20 years ago. Research at that time had indicated that the average mind of a person has over 63,000 thoughts going through it every 24-hour day. I'm guessing with today's "information age" and a much higher level of social media interaction, the typical mind is dealing with a much higher volume of daily thoughts in this era. That said, our mind is a powerful tool that is "bombarded" with enormous quantities of simple and complex stimuli that we continuously have to sort out.

When I run, I focus my mind on the conditions, elements, variables, and circumstances of the moment and on God helping me through those. I feel He gives me the challenges I need at each moment and then partners with me to navigate through them the best way possible. To help my focus on God and these areas of concern, I prefer to run "wireless," with no ancillary devices. Most runners I've observed prefer some level of electronics, and some have told me that boredom sets in for them if they don't have their music or other programming available.

I want to be as totally aware of my surroundings as I possibly can be. This allows me to be "in tune" with and to "listen" to God and His created natural settings. I am also able to hear and sense animals, birds, breezes, and motorized vehicles. From my experience, when I run towards another walker or runner, who is "wired," and say a friendly, "Good morning," for example, it appears that their audio stimuli have captured their focus, and its volume prevents the comprehension of my voice.

Although I choose not to take music of any sort with me on a running journey, all is not quiet for me on a typical run. For motivational purposes, there are several catch phrases or mottos that I say or sing that help me during challenging times. When I'm doing hill training, I use the thought, "Tame the beast," to help me conquer an incline. Another self-created slogan is, "Power pistons pounding," reminding myself to use my arms like pistons to help me set a consistent rhythm. Frequently, as a mindset, I eliminate the thoughts of going uphill and downhill, but instead use directional terms like, "I'm running north right now," for example, and telling myself that all pavement is flat. If I get into a good pace that I want to keep, regardless of whether I'm running left, right, up or down, I simply repeat, "left foot, right foot." This helps me put the emphasis on one step at a time in rhythm and not to focus on the elevation of the hill.

Running downhill, especially on a steep decline, also presents a challenge. The body, and sometimes the mind and spirit, want to take advantage of gravity and turn a jog or run into an all-out sprint. The potential for injury—like a muscle pull or strain, a twisted knee, or sprained ankle—is definitely enhanced. An accelerated pace can easily change my posture and structural alignment, as well as my stride and overall efficiency of movement. My goal during these moments is to hold my pace and posture in check and not increase my speed, at least not significantly. So that word, "hold," becomes my motto, for both uphill and downhill running. *Can I hold my body parts and pace together, even though my stride is a little shorter and my body wants to run slower going up a hill? Can I also do it when my body wants a much longer stride and prefers racing down a hill?*

Using the word "hold" helps me with patience also. The hill is merely a temporary challenge, and I should not rush its completion. When I continue to say that word, it reminds me of a scene from the Hollywood movie, *Braveheart*. Mel Gibson's Scottish freedom fighter, William Wallace, encourages his remarkably out-numbered "army" of commoners to hold their position with unbelievable patience as the fast-charging enemy on horses nears his foot-soldiers. With defeat and possible demise staring each warrior right in the face, they must be patient until precisely the right moment to launch their surprise, strategic, and successful counter-attack.

"Patient endurance is what you need now,
so that you will continue to do God's will.
Then you will receive all that he has promised."
HEBREWS 10:36

Another mindset and visual that I use is "Tall Kenyan." Some of the smoothest and most efficient and successful runners on the planet are native Kenyans. I have an enormous amount of respect for their dedication to distance running and to their proper alignment of body mechanics. I love watching their precision movements on TV or on a video screen at a race in which I am also entered. They usually finish their race before I start mine, since elite and world-class runners take off first to avoid any crowds of fellow participants. My phrase reminds me to try to run as body-efficient as they do, with an apparent calmness and relaxed limbs.

Also, I'm reminded to stay as upright with my posture as I can, as I frequently have a "stooped-over" look, due to my rounded upper back. This is definitely a challenge for me later in a race as fatigue sets in, gravity takes over, and tension builds up at the acupressure points at the upper tips of both of my shoulder blades.

For my lower body, whenever my posture, stride—or both—change negatively, I have another thought pattern I use. This emphasizes four words that begin with the letter "S." I try to keep my feet, ankles, knees, and hips in proper alignment with these words: "Strong, stable, steady, and solid." I hope my toes are pointed straight ahead, the mid-foot strikes the pavement, and my lead foot is under my chest. During any run there are many check points, especially for an older runner. I try my best to not only listen to my body and all of its parts, but I also listen to God and His guidance for me.

Whether I'm running a "beast" of a hill, trying to emulate a world-class runner, focusing on patience, form, or the next step, through it all I have God beside me. Regardless of which mindset or catch phrase I use for a given run or race, I simply add, *With You, God*. Sometimes, that's all I need to say when a challenge arises.

> *"Don't be afraid, for I am with you. Don't be discouraged,*
> *for I am your God. I will strengthen you and help you . . ."*
>
> ISAIAH 41:10

Marathon Motivation

After I ran a half marathon (13.1 miles) race in Fort Wayne one year, my son Kerry made the observation, "Hey Dad, you did a half marathon at the age of 60, so are you going to run a full marathon at age 70, ha ha!" At the time, he thought I was already stretching life a bit too far after only a few years of running, and then he added a little humor on top of that.

Well, I took his comments as motivation, as part of the spiritual component of mind-body-spirit balance, and I actually got into full marathon mode much sooner than his humor implied. After I completed a half marathon in the fall of 2012, I slowly increased my mileage to the point where I was able to run and finish a full marathon in Florida in January 2013—about three and a half months later. Instead of waiting until age seventy, as our son quipped, I accomplished this personal running milestone soon before the age of sixty-three.

I was definitely a "happy camper" to run those 26-plus miles with God's help with hydration, nutrition, and overall survival of the conditions. Adding to the euphoric finish was seeing Cathy and her homemade sign of encouragement near the end, five and three-quarters hours after I started. Contributing also to the conclusion of that once-in-a-lifetime running adventure was a 15- to 20-member, robed choral group, who sang the spiritual song, "Halleluiah." The talented harmonizers stood on concert risers as I passed by and finished my final minute of running. *What a memorable and uplifting experience that was for a tired and depleted body!* It was a true moment of Holy Spiritual running and life bliss!

A Little Extra

Whether I finish a long or short race or a purposeful training run, my goal is to do a little more at the end. For a race, it is recommended that runners continue to keep moving, albeit much slower or even walking, to help with the transition from activity to non-activity mode. For a training run, it is usually a little extra distance or time. It could be as simple as running to the next traffic sign, telephone pole, or intersection, or by adding another minute or two. God is always with me to the end of a run, as my motto reminds me: "Trust God, just do it." I am thankful for these positive endings, as every run has a purpose, such as training for variables such as heat, humidity, elevation, distance, or speed.

Going the Distance with God

As stated before, I endeavored on my first Peachtree Road Race on July 4, 2006, almost one year to the day after my running mentor's passing in mid-July 2005. This experience ended in the medical tent, fortunately with a positive result, thanks to

God's intervention and expert care from the trained staff. Surviving all of that, I added God more profoundly to my daily life and certainly even more so to my running life.

With different training methods and running gear, a new training pathway, and of course, taking God along, my running life took on a more defined meaning and purpose. Despite the trauma from the year before, I was able to return to the Atlanta race the next year. I was definitely on a mission to get to that finish line under my own power and cross it in a vertical position this time. With marked improvements in *every* phase of my running life, my time for the race was four minutes faster than the estimated time the year before.

Although I continued my running life, other circumstances didn't allow me to make the trip to Atlanta to do that race again until 2016. Since then, I've been able to run that race each year, and I hope to again this year. Each of the past four years, I've sensed His presence helping me to overcome running issues—including a tight calf muscle, a tender hamstring, or plantar fasciitis—to help get me to the finish line on each occasion. My times during that span have been consistently between 66 and 69 minutes with no trauma drama at the finish line.

Meanwhile, up north, with a totally new outlook on life and running, I started doing the fall Fort Wayne race in 2009. At that time, only two races were available, and I chose the half marathon (13.1 miles) for participation. I continued doing that same race in the fall for the next four years as well. For those longer races, I followed two convictions without compromise: I stayed in tune with God and stopped at every water station for hydration!

As mentioned previously, I ventured into one and only one full marathon in Florida in early 2013. Again, with lessons learned, there were 20 water stops over the 26 miles, and I stopped at *every one of them!* I also paused my run four times for nutrition and four times for simple medical attention. There I applied liniment to aching back, shoulder, and leg areas, which kept my body moving forward and got me to the finish line.

The longer races are totally in my past now, as I have aged and prefer to spend less time training for races and more time doing other activities in life. My running diet now includes only the two 10K races and a few 5K adventures each year, when I am healthy. For an added challenge, only once annually I sign up for both races on the same day, again, when good health allows. Whether it's a long or short training run or race, I stay in tune with God as my running partner and listen to Him as best I can.

". . . And let us run with endurance the race
God has set before us."

Hebrews 12:1

CONVERSING WITH GOD

10

Next Step

At our church, one of the on-going themes for spiritual growth is taking that "next step" with one's relationship with God. It doesn't matter on what step you presently reside, or if you have taken any steps in that direction, there is always a next step. In general, my everyday step is to be constantly aware of my surroundings and circumstances and serve as many people as I can, as often as I can. In addition to melding running with God's presence, writing this manuscript has been a surprisingly big next step for me.

For conversation starters that give me a relaxed, comfortable beginning to a run or race, I use phrases like, "With You, God," "In Your hands, God," "We can do this," or, "Let's do this." Later during my journey, whenever appropriate, I say, "Thank You for these variables (i.e., hills, wind, heat, humidity)," "Whatever You give me is what I need at this moment," "Help me find a way to do my best right now," "Thank You, God, for the opportunity to run with You," "Thank You for helping me complete that last mile," "We've got a tough challenge today," "I need a little help with this one, God," or, "One step at a time with You, God."

I make sure God is with me, whenever I put on my running shoes. I try to keep Him as my anchor not only when I do my normal everyday activities, but also when I run my miles. In addition to helping me finish runs and races when I was fairly healthy, He has given me the necessary guidance to finish what I've started when I wasn't injury-free (i.e., plantar fasciitis, jammed toe, strained calf muscle, pulled hamstring muscle, cracked ribs). I take this philosophy: *Run with Him. Put Him first, and follow His guidance.* This usually eases my discomfort, helps me relax, and lets God show me the way with His plan.

> *"Spiritual people are not those who*
> *engage in certain spiritual practices;*
> *they are those who draw their life*
> *from a conversational relationship with God."*
> DALLAS WILLARD, American Philosopher

EPILOGUE

Playing It Forward

If you are looking to start something new, whether in general or in the fitness world, start with that first step, as slow as it needs to be. Then take that second step and continue, one at a time, left foot, right foot, etc. After a few more, turn the corner onto Auburn Drive, another street, a country road, or simply, through an open door, and say, *Good morning, God! Here I am, one of Your children.* With that, you will add a new, personal walking-running "partner" and an eternal friend.

"Run" with God and let His Holy Spirit into your life to motivate your spirit with passion, strengthen your body physically, and calm, clear, and open your mind to His will. May God bless you on your journey, run with you, and turn your miles into smiles for Him and you!

Final Thoughts

As I put my last entry into this undertaking, I stand ready to see what the upcoming running-racing season and next decade of life will bring me. My next race is only a few days away, and when I step across that start line, I will have celebrated seventy years completed on this planet. Last year was my best year ever as far as being able to run all six races for which I registered. I felt blessed to run healthily and competitively for all six of them. The year before, I was only able to finish four races.

Regardless of the quantity or quality of my races for this year, I begin my season with the confidence of God's presence at my side. The gifts and talents He has given me and His will determine how my season progresses and finishes. Each step is a blessing that I never take for granted.

While God continues to bless me with health good enough to continue running, I'm sure that as I age, doing my best will simply be getting to and through a finish line. And that, too, will bring a smile to my face. Running with God, on a course or not, moment-by-moment, day-by-day, is something I'll continue until my body is not physically able, or when my Heavenly Father calls me home. Like many of you, I am a child of God.

"For you are all children of God through faith."

GALATIANS 3:26

For each of you, I hope that you can seek, find, and trust God to help you through your many life endeavors, including moving at whatever level you are capable. May you enjoy "running" with God and be at peace.

INSPIRATIONS

Praise God for His ongoing presence in my life and for His urgings for me to write this book.

Heartfelt thanks extend to my wife, Cathy, for her patience, spiritual encouragement, and assistance with Scripture research and photography editing. Sincere thanks go to longtime friend of nearly fifty years and editor of *The Star*, Dave Kurtz, for his inspiration and assistance with research and photography.

I wish to also thank my former high school student and now author and founder of Restoration Road Ministries, Dr. Mitch Kruse, for inspirational stories and weekly devotionals. Also, I extend a thank you to pastors Steve Buckner and Bill Lyne, present and past Lead Pastors at Dayspring Community Church for their deep passion to share God's Word with meaningful messages.

Additional inspiration has come from *Hour of Power with Pastor Bobby Schuller,* and from the daily devotional book *Strength for the Day: 365 Devotions.*

To all of God's messengers on my daily trail of life, I offer my deepest appreciation for giving me abundantly more than you will ever realize. I continue to see God's presence through you.